Celebrate the Months
DECEMBER

EDITOR:

Kristine Johnson

ILLUSTRATORS:

Dave Christensen

Darcy Tom

Jane Yamada

PROJECT DIRECTOR:

Carolea Williams

CONTRIBUTING WRITERS:

Trisha Callella	Ronda Howley
Rosa Drew	Kim Jordano
Marguerite Duke	Mary Kurth

TABLE OF CONTENTS

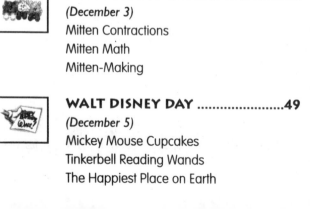

INTRODUCTION

Seasons, holidays, annual events, and just-for-fun monthly themes provide fitting frameworks for learning! Celebrate December and its special days with these exciting and unique activities. This activity book of integrated curriculum ideas includes the following:

MONTHLY CELEBRATION THEMES

▲ **monthly celebration activities** that relate to monthlong events or themes: Christmas around the World, Jolly Santa, and Snowmen.

▲ **literature lists** of fiction and nonfiction books for each monthly celebration.

▲ **bulletin-board displays** that can be used for seasonal decoration and interactive learning-center fun.

▲ **take-home activities** to reinforce what is being taught in school, encourage home–school communication, and help children connect home and school learning.

SPECIAL-DAY THEMES

▲ **special-day activities** that relate to 15 special December days, including Deck the Halls Day, Winter Solstice, and Make-a-Gift Day. Activities integrate art, songs and chants, language arts, math, science, and social studies.

▲ **calendar cards** that complement each of the 15 special days and add some extra seasonal fun to your daily calendar time.

▲ **literature lists** of fiction and nonfiction books for each special day.

FUN FORMS

▲ a **blank monthly calendar** for writing lesson plans, dates to remember, special events, book titles, new words, and incentives, or for math and calendar activities.

▲ a **seasonal border page** that adds eye-catching appeal to parent notes, homework assignments, letters, certificates, announcements, and bulletins.

▲ a **seasonal journal page** for students to share thoughts, feelings, stories, or experiences. Reproduce and bind several pages for individual journals or combine single, completed journal pages to make a class book.

▲ a **classroom newsletter** for students to report current classroom events and share illustrations, comics, stories, or poems. Reproduce and send completed newsletters home to keep families informed and involved.

▲ **clip art** to add a seasonal flair to bulletin boards, class projects, charts, and parent notes.

SPECIAL-DAY CALENDAR CARD ACTIVITIES

Below are a variety of ways to introduce special-day calendar cards into your curriculum.

PATTERNING

During daily calendar time, use one of these patterning activities to reinforce students' math skills.

▲ Use special-day calendar cards and your own calendar markers to create a pattern for the month, such as regular day, regular day, special day.

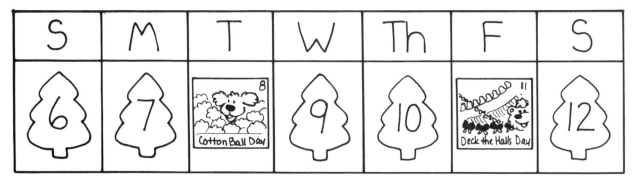

▲ Number special-day cards in advance. Use only even- or odd-numbered special days for patterning. (Create your own "special days" with the blank calendar cards.) Use your own calendar markers to create the other half of the pattern.

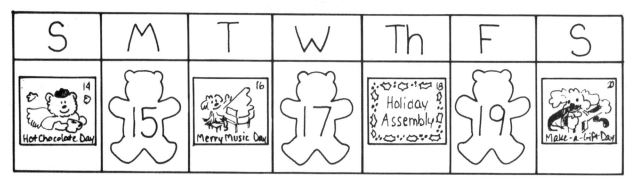

▲ At the beginning of the month, attach the special-day cards to the calendar. Use your own calendar markers for patterning. When a special day arrives, invite a student to remove the special-day card and replace it with your calendar marker to continue the pattern.

HIDE AND FIND

On the first day of the month, hide numbered special-day cards around the classroom. Invite students to find them and bring them to the calendar area. Have a student volunteer hang each card in the correct calendar space as you explain the card's significance.

A FESTIVE INTRODUCTION

On the first day of the month, display numbered special-day cards in a festive setting, such as hanging the cards on an evergreen tree. Invite students, one at a time, to remove a card and attach it to the calendar as you explain its significance.

POCKET-CHART SENTENCE STRIPS

Have the class dictate a sentence to correspond with each special-day card. Write the sentences on individual sentence strips. For example, on Gingerbread Day you might write *On this special day, we make gingerbread men.* Put the sentence strips away. When a special day arrives, place the corresponding strip in a pocket chart next to the calendar. Move a fun "pointer" (such as a gingerbread pattern attached to the end of a yardstick) under the words, and have students read the sentence aloud. Add sentences to the pocket chart on each special day.

GUESS WHAT I HAVE

Discuss the special days and give each student a photocopy of one special-day card. (Two or three students may have the same card.) Have students take turns describing their cards without revealing the special day, such as *This is the day we celebrate the animals that pull Santa's sleigh.* Invite the student who guesses Reindeer Day to attach the card to the calendar.

TREAT BAGS

Place each special-day card and a small corresponding treat or prize in a resealable plastic bag. For example, place a package of instant hot cocoa in a bag for Hot Chocolate Day. On the first day of the month, pin the bags on a bulletin board near the calendar. Remove the cards from the bags and attach them to the calendar as you discuss each day. As a special day arrives, remove the corresponding bag's contents and discuss them. Choose a student to keep the contents as a special reward.

LITERATURE MATCHUP

Have students sit in two lines facing each other. Provide the members of one group with special-day cards and the members of the other group with books whose subjects match the special-day cards held by the other group. Invite students to match cards and books, come forward in pairs, and introduce the day and book. Display the books near the calendar for students to read.

MINI-BOOKS

Reproduce numbered special-day cards so each student has a set. Have students sequence and staple their cards to make mini-books. Invite students to read their books and take them home to share with family members.

CREATIVE WRITING

Have each student glue a copy of a special-day card to a piece of construction paper. Invite students to illustrate and write about their special day. Have students share their writing. Display the writing near the calendar.

LUNCH SACK GAME

Provide each student with a paper lunch sack, a photocopy of each special-day card, and 15 index cards. Have students decorate the sacks for the month. Invite students to color the special-day cards and write on separate index cards a word or sentence describing each day. Have students place the special-day cards and index cards in the sacks. Ask students to trade sacks, empty the contents, and match index cards to special-day cards.

SPECIAL-DAY BOX

One week before a special day, provide each student with a photocopied special-day card, an empty check box or shoebox, and a four-page square blank book. Ask each student to take the box, book, and card home to prepare a special-day box presentation. Have students write about their special day on the four book pages and place in the box small pictures or artifacts relating to the day. Ask students to decorate the boxes and glue their special-day cards to the top. Have students bring the completed boxes to school on the special day and give their presentations as an introduction to the day.

CHRISTMAS AROUND THE WORLD

Christmas is truly an international holiday. Encourage students to share their family traditions and learn about Christmas traditions in other countries. Each day, teach students about a new country and how they celebrate the winter holidays. Locate the country on a map; study a traditional custom; prepare a special holiday food; do an art project; and read a story from or about the country.

LITERATURE LINKS

Christmas All Over
by Robert Bernardini

The Christmas Ark
by Robert D. San Souci

Christmas around the World
by Emily Kelley

Christmas around the World
by Mary D. Lankford

The Fir Tree
by Hans Christian Andersen

Nine Days to Christmas
by Marie Hall Ets

Pancho's Piñata
by Stefan Czernecki

CHRISTMAS AROUND THE WORLD BULLETIN BOARD

Cut a large butcher paper circle. Paint the circle to look like a globe. When the paint dries, create a three-dimensional effect by stuffing newspaper under the globe while you staple it around its perimeter to a bulletin board. Invite students to work in groups "dressing" international paper dolls in their traditional costumes. Place the paper dolls around the globe. For each doll, write on a sentence strip the name of the country the doll represents, and attach the strip below the doll.

MATERIALS
▲ butcher paper
▲ scissors
▲ green and blue paint/paintbrushes
▲ stapler
▲ newspaper
▲ crayons or markers
▲ sentence strips

CHRISTMAS COOKBOOK

Ask students to seek help from their families to find a holiday recipe from another country and bring it to class. Have students write their name next to the recipe and draw a picture of the food. Make copies of the recipes and bind them into international cookbooks for each student to take home.

MATERIALS
▲ construction paper
▲ crayons or markers
▲ glue
▲ pine tree branches
▲ bark
▲ candy
▲ tea bags
▲ flower petals
▲ felt
▲ bookbinding materials

THE DAYS OF WINTER

Invite each student to create an international holiday book. Each day, study the holiday customs of a different place, and have students write the frame *On the _____ day of winter, my good friend gave to me _____.* Have students fill in the day and a traditional holiday item from that country, such as an item from the list below. Students can draw pictures of the items and/or glue on actual items. For example, students can glue on a pine branch for the Tannenbaum, a piece of bark for the Yule log, a piece of candy for the piñata, a tea bag for the tea and sweet roll, a flower petal for the lei, or a tiny felt stocking for the stocking. Have students write on the last page *On the _____ day of winter, we had a party to celebrate all these countries.* Invite students to sing the lines from their book to the tune of "The 12 Days of Christmas."

a Tannenbaum from Germany
a Yule log from England
a piñata from Mexico
a sweet roll and tea from Sweden
a Nativity scene from France
a flower lei from Hawaii
a Dutch clog from the Netherlands
a stocking from the U.S.A.

SMALL-WORLD PROGRAM

Have student groups choose a country to study for a small-world program. Invite each group to learn a song or dance from the country, make a costume from that country to wear, and decorate a life-size paper doll dressed in the country's traditional dress. Students will enjoy tasting foods from the culture and looking at artifacts, maps, and pictures of the area. Have students sing "Hello from All the Children of the World" and then perform their song or dance for family members or other classes. Invite a student volunteer to end the program by saying *We have our own small world right here in the United States, with cultures and customs from every place.*

MATERIALS
▲ butcher paper
▲ crayons, markers, or paint/paintbrushes
▲ maps
▲ "Hello from All the Children of the World" from *Wee Sing around the World*

TRAVELING BOOK BAG

HOME ACTIVITY

Send home with a different student each night a canvas tote bag containing a storybook about holiday traditions, a world map, and a blank journal. Write a note to the family members asking them to read the book with their child, write in the journal where their relatives came from and what holiday traditions they celebrate, and locate on the map their relatives' countries of origin.

MATERIALS
▲ canvas tote bag
▲ storybook about holiday traditions
▲ world map
▲ blank journal
▲ family letter

GERMANY

The Christmas season in Germany begins with the beginning of Advent, the fourth Sunday prior to Christmas Day. The Advent calendar, a calendar with windows used to count down the days until Christmas, originated in Germany. Some say the Christmas tree comes from Germany. Legend tells us that Martin Luther was walking through the forest on Christmas Eve and saw the stars shining through the trees. He thought it was so beautiful that he cut down a tree and decorated it with candles. The Christmas tree's wood represents peace and its evergreen branches represent eternal life. In many German cities, special markets with decorated booths are set up for weeks before Christmas. Only items related to Christmas may be offered for sale. The Christmas Market in Nuremberg, which has existed for over 400 years, is the most famous. Many German Christians attend midnight mass on Christmas Eve.

GERMAN TANNENBAUM HATS

Read aloud *The Fir Tree*. Discuss the origin of the Tannenbaum (Christmas tree). Have students trace the Tannenbaum pattern on green construction paper and cut it out. Invite students to decorate the tree with glitter, sequins, stickers, or holiday gift wrap. Have students glue their tree to the center of a sentence strip. Staple the sentence strip ends so they fit around each student's head. Invite students to wear their Tannenbaum hats while singing "O Tannenbaum" ("Oh, Christmas Tree").

MATERIALS

▲ *The Fir Tree* by Hans Christian Andersen
▲ Tannenbaum pattern (page 20)
▲ green construction paper
▲ scissors
▲ glue
▲ art supplies (crayons, markers, glitter, sequins, stickers, holiday wrapping paper)
▲ sentence strips
▲ stapler

ADVENT CALENDAR

The Advent calendar is a German tradition. People use the calendar to count the days until Christmas. To make a unique class Advent calendar, paint a paper plate and 24 film canisters or matchboxes gold. Number the canisters from 1 to 24 with a silver marker. Invite each student to take home a canister or matchbox and fill it with a special treat, prize, or drawing of something meaningful about the season. Punch holes around the plate rim and tie gold curling ribbon to the holes. Gather the ribbon at the top, knot it, and hang the plate from the ceiling. Tie different lengths of gold curling ribbon to the rim and tie or tape the canisters to the ends. Each day of the month, invite a student to cut the string that corresponds to the date and open the canister to find a special treat.

MATERIALS

▲ paper plate
▲ gold paint
▲ 24 film canisters or matchboxes
▲ silver marker
▲ hole punch
▲ gold curling ribbon
▲ tape

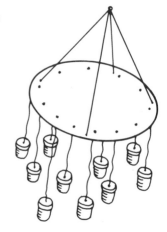

ENGLAND

Many prevailing American Christmas traditions derive from English Christmas traditions. In England, children believe Father Christmas comes dressed in a red suit and hat on Christmas Eve and delivers toys and gifts to children. Children write letters to Father Christmas, but instead of mailing the letters, they drop them in the fireplace and Father Christmas reads the smoke. People began to hang stockings by the fireplace because they believed Father Christmas dropped gold coins down the chimney into a stocking. Children continue to hang stockings, hoping to find them filled with gifts. The English decorate their homes with holly and ivy as a reminder that spring is not far off. The English have been decorating trees since 1841, when Prince Albert set up a Christmas tree for his wife Victoria and their children.

ENGLISH PARTY POPPERS

Party poppers or "Christmas crackers" originated in the 1800s in England. Party poppers are gifts with fancy wrappings that pop with a crack when pulled in half. Invite students to make their own version of party poppers. Have students place a small prize inside a small cardboard tube, wrap the tube in tissue paper, and tie the ends with ribbon. Invite students to decorate the party popper with stickers and give it to a friend.

MATERIALS
▲ small cardboard tubes
▲ small prizes (marbles, jacks, drawings, stickers)
▲ tissue paper
▲ ribbon
▲ stickers

HERE'S TO GOOD HEALTH!

The word *wassail* is a toast to good health. Wassail is also a beverage made of mulled ale, curdled cream, roasted apples, eggs, cloves, ginger, nutmeg, and sugar. It is served from huge bowls. Make a version of wassail for your students. In a slow cooker, add apple cider, a few cinnamon sticks, nutmeg, and a sliced orange. Heat for a few hours and serve heated in Styrofoam bowls. Invite students to drink from the bowls for a hot holiday treat.

MATERIALS
▲ slow cooker
▲ apple cider
▲ cinnamon sticks
▲ nutmeg
▲ sliced orange
▲ Styrofoam bowls

MEXICO

Las Posadas *(the inns)*, a Christmas tradition celebrated in Mexico, begins nine days before Christmas. The nine days represent Mary and Joseph's original nine-day journey from Nazareth to Bethlehem. On each of the nine days, families led by children parade down the streets singing carols. They travel from house to house pretending to look for an inn to shelter Mary and Joseph. They are refused at each house until they reach the house where a Nativity and altar are set up and everyone is invited inside. There they celebrate with prayer, a feast, dancing, and the breaking of a piñata.

MEXICAN STAR PIÑATAS

Read aloud *Pancho's Piñata* about the first piñata. Invite each student to color and cut out two copies of the Star reproducible. Have students glue the stars to either side of a paper lunch sack. Invite students to fill the sacks with candy and tie them closed with yarn. Students can take their star piñatas home to break them with their family members.

MATERIALS
▲ *Pancho's Piñata* by Stefan Czernecki
▲ Star reproducible (page 21)
▲ scissors
▲ crayons or markers
▲ glue
▲ paper lunch sacks
▲ candy
▲ yarn

MUSICAL MARACAS

Invite each student to decorate the bottom side of two paper plates. Have students put beans on one plate, place a tongue depressor perpendicular to the rim, and cover the beans with the other plate. Help students staple the plates together around the rim to make maracas. Invite students to hold their maracas by the handle and shake them while they sing "The Piñata Song."

MATERIALS
▲ small paper plates
▲ dried beans
▲ stapler
▲ markers
▲ tongue depressors

The Piñata Song
(to the tune of "Pop Goes the Weasel")

I'm a little star piñata,
Hanging from a tree.
Children hit me with a bat,
And treats pop out of me!

BUÑELOS

MATERIALS

▲ flour tortillas
▲ vegetable oil
▲ electric skillet
▲ paper sacks
▲ cinnamon
▲ sugar

For a yummy Mexican holiday treat, make buñelos. Add vegetable oil to an electric skillet. Deep-fry flour tortillas in the hot oil. Set them on paper towels to cool. Pour cinnamon and sugar into a paper sack. Place the flour tortillas one at a time in the sack and invite students to shake the sack. Enjoy!

SILENT NIGHT

Teach your students how to sing "Silent Night" in English, Spanish, and French. Perform the song for other classes.

Silent Night

Silent night, holy night.
All is calm. All is bright.
'Round yon virgin, mother and child.
Holy infant so tender and mild.
Sleep in heavenly peace.
Sleep in heavenly peace.

Noche de paz, noche de amor.
Todo duerme en derredor
Entre sus astros que esparcen su luz.
Bella anunciando al niñito Jesús.
Brilla la estrella de paz,
Brilla la estrella de paz.

Douce nuit, sainte nuit.
Le hameau dort sans bruit.
Dans l'étable repose un enfant
Que sa mère contemple en priant.
Elle a vu le Saveur
Dans l'enfant de son cœur.

SWEDEN

Saint Lucia Day is celebrated in Sweden on December 13th. St. Lucia, a 4th-century saint, is said to have carried food to Christians hiding in dark underground tunnels. To light the way, she wore a wreath of candles on her head. Early in the morning the eldest daughter, dressed in a white gown with a red sash and a crown of evergreen and seven lighted candles, awakens each family member with a traditional song, hot coffee or tea, and sweet buns. *Lucia* means *light* and Swedes believe St. Lucia welcomes the Christmas season. The children believe that on Christmas Eve a Christmas gnome, *Tomte*, comes from under the house and leaves gifts for everyone.

SWEDISH STAR-BOY HATS

Have each boy in the class roll a large piece of construction paper into a cone shape and staple it closed to make a pointed hat. Invite boys to decorate their hat with construction-paper stars and other art supplies. Have boys wear their hats for the Crowns of Light activity (below).

MATERIALS
- ▲ 12" x 18" (30.5 cm x 46 cm) white construction paper
- ▲ stapler
- ▲ construction-paper stars
- ▲ art supplies (glitter, glue, sequins)

CROWNS OF LIGHT

Fit green construction-paper strips around each girl's head and staple the ends to form an "evergreen crown." Invite girls to glue on fringed green paper. Have girls cut out the candles from the reproducible and color bright-colored flames. Students can glue the candles around the crown. Invite students to role-play the Saint Lucia tradition and serve tea and sweet rolls to classmates.

MATERIALS
- ▲ Candles reproducible (page 22)
- ▲ 2" x 18" (5 cm x 46 cm) green construction-paper strips
- ▲ stapler
- ▲ scissors
- ▲ glue
- ▲ crayons or markers
- ▲ tea
- ▲ sweet rolls
- ▲ cups, plates, and napkins

NETHERLANDS

St. Nicholas Day, brought to America by Dutch settlers, is celebrated on December 6. St. Nicholas, known as *Sinterklaas* in the Netherlands, was a real person born over 1600 years ago who became the patron saint of children because of his many acts of kindness and generosity. He gave food, clothes, and toys to poor children. He did not want them to be embarassed by his gifts, so he gave them secretly. Dutch children fill their shoes with hay and sugar for St. Nicholas's horse and awake to find their shoes filled with gifts such as nuts or candy on the morning of St. Nicholas Day.

DUTCH CLOGS

Have students color and cut out the Dutch Clog reproducible, fold it on the dotted line, and staple it along the sides. Invite students to put Spanish moss or raffia in their clogs and leave them on their desks at the end of the day. After students go home, replace the Spanish moss or raffia with treats such as stickers or candy.

MATERIALS
▲ Dutch Clog reproducible (page 23)
▲ crayons or markers
▲ scissors
▲ stapler
▲ Spanish moss or raffia
▲ treats (stickers or candy)

HOLIDAY HORNS

The people of Twente in East Holland hold a ceremony in which special horns are blown to chase away evil spirits and to announce the birth of Christ. The horns are made from 3'–4' (1 m) saplings. They sound a deep tone, similar to a foghorn. To make their own special horns, students can each decorate a long cardboard gift-wrap tube. Encourage students to use their imagination as they make festive decorations on the tube. Invite students to blow their horns all at once for a booming announcement!

MATERIALS
▲ cardboard gift-wrap tubes
▲ art supplies (paint/paintbrushes, crayons, markers, stickers, gift wrap, glitter, yarn, ribbon, sequins, etc.)

FRANCE

Nearly every French home displays a Nativity scene, or *crèche*. Many families build their own crèche, and French children set it up after hearing the Christmas story. The *crèche* often includes clay figures called *santons* or "little saints," which include Mary, Joseph, baby Jesus, shepherds, the Magi, and sometimes local dignitaries. *Père Noël*, Father Christmas, is accompanied by his companion *Père Fouettard*, who reminds *Père Noël* of how each child has behaved. *Père Noël* brings small gifts on December 6 and returns on Christmas to bring more. French children leave their shoes by the fireplace in hopes that *Père Noël* or *Petit Jesu* (Little Jesus) will place gifts there for them. The French also have a feast after midnight mass on Christmas Eve called *le réveillon.*

FRENCH NATIVITY SCENE

Invite students to create clay figures, including the baby Jesus, the wise men, Mary, and Joseph, for a Nativity scene. Have students use fabric scraps to dress the figures. Have students lay the baby Jesus on Spanish moss and wrap him in cheesecloth. Have students decorate the inside of a shoe box to resemble a stable and place the figures inside.

MATERIALS
▲ clay
▲ shoe boxes
▲ art supplies (Spanish moss, craft sticks, fabric scraps, cheesecloth, construction paper, glue, scissors)

WHAT DID THE ANIMALS THINK?

Invite students to draw a picture of the baby Jesus in a manger with animals around him. Then have students look at the scene from the animals' perspective and write in speech bubbles the animals' reactions to the newborn baby.

MATERIALS
▲ construction paper
▲ art supplies (crayons, markers, pastels, or paint/paintbrushes)

HAWAII

Mele Kalikimaka! (Merry Christmas, as they say in sunny Hawaii.) Hawaiian children celebrate Christmas much the same as other American children, but the weather is often warmer and the Christmas trees are often different. Palm trees are frequently decorated for Christmas, especially in outdoor displays and neighborhood yards. Some Hawaiians show Santa riding an outrigger with dolphins instead of a sleigh with reindeer and elves dressed in aloha shirts. Celebrations are always a little different in Hawaii, but where else but the Big Island can someone snowboard down icy slopes in the morning and surf in warm waters that same afternoon?

HAWAIIAN LEIS

Invite students to celebrate Christmas Hawaiian style. Help students hole-punch the center of construction-paper flower shapes. Have students string (in a pattern) packing bubbles, colored macaroni, and the circles on yarn to make Hawaiian leis. Invite students to wear the leis throughout the day.

MATERIALS
- ▲ hole punch
- ▲ construction-paper flower shapes
- ▲ packing bubbles
- ▲ yarn
- ▲ colored macaroni

MY HAWAIIAN CHRISTMAS

Invite students to draw a large palm tree on construction paper. Ask students to write and draw on the palm tree something from Hawaii they would like to give or receive, such as a hula skirt, banana, or surfboard.

MATERIALS
- ▲ construction paper
- ▲ crayons or markers

Curtis

I would like a surfboard from Hawaii.

TANNENBAUM

December © 1998 Creative Teaching Press

STAR

CANDLES

Christmas around the World

DUTCH CLOG

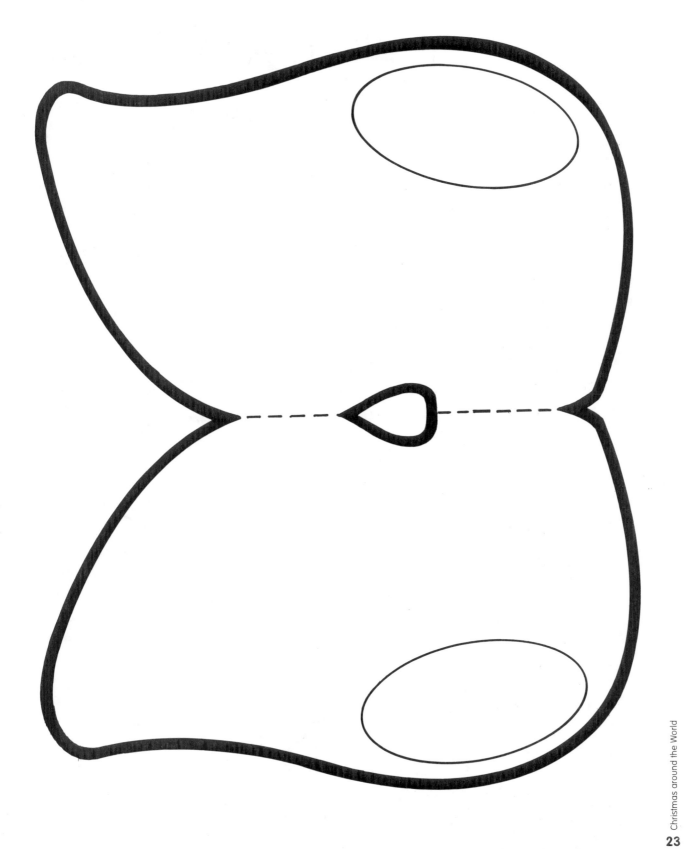

JOLLY SANTA

Santa Claus, Jolly old St. Nicholas, or Father Christmas, whatever name he goes by, always brings smiles and giggles to young faces. Celebrate the joy and laughter that accompanies Santa. Ho—Ho—Hope you have a great time!

LITERATURE LINKS

Arthur's Christmas
by Marc Brown

The Bear Santa Claus Forgot
by Diana Kimpton

Christmas Eve at Santa's
by Alf Prysen

*Dear Santa: Please Don't
Come This Year*
by Patricia D. Ludlow

Fat Santa
by Margery Cuyler

Father Christmas
by Raymond Briggs

Jolly Old Santa Claus
by Alice Leedy Mason

Santa's Book of Names
by David Mc Phail

Santa's Favorite Story
by Hisako Aoki

LOOK WHO'S COMING DOWN THE CHIMNEY BULLETIN BOARD

Invite students to help create a butcher-paper chimney on a bulletin board. Cut out large butcher-paper boots, cover them with black trash bags for a shiny effect, and attach them below the chimney. Have students each draw a self-portrait on large construction paper to create a "family portrait." Create a frame around the picture. Invite students to make the Holiday Stockings on page 78. Then students can hang their stocking on the chimney. Title the bulletin board *Dropping by with a Christmas "Hi!"* Invite students to sing "Santa Is Coming" and then encourage them to make up their own verses.

MATERIALS
▲ butcher paper
▲ paint/paintbrushes
▲ black trash bags
▲ crayons or markers
▲ construction paper
▲ scissors

Santa Is Coming
(to the tune of "She'll Be Comin' 'round the Mountain")

He'll be coming down the chimney when he comes.
He'll be coming down the chimney when he comes.
He'll be coming down the chimney.
He'll be coming down the chimney.
He'll be coming down the chimney when he comes.

SANTA MOBILES

Trace Santa Mobile patterns on construction paper, one set of patterns for each student. Instruct students to cut out the patterns. Have students glue the beard to the bottom of the hat. Invite students to glue cotton balls to the beard. Ask students to glue construction-paper strips to make stripes across the hat and glue construction-paper eyes from the brim of the hat so they dangle below. Hang the Santa mobiles from the ceiling by fishing wire.

MATERIALS

▲ Santa Mobile patterns (pages 29 and 30)
▲ red, green, yellow, and white construction paper
▲ scissors
▲ glue
▲ cotton balls
▲ fishing wire

SANTA WORK SACKS

On the day before winter vacation, invite students to prepare a "Santa Work Sack" for a secret pal. Have students include in their sack different activities for their secret pals, such as puzzles, cartoons, original dot-to-dot pictures, mazes, math problems, map questions, sentences to finish, or doodles to complete. Hold a name drawing at the end of the day and distribute the Santa work sacks.

MATERIALS

▲ paper sacks
▲ paper
▲ art supplies

Jolly Santa

SANTA'S HELPER REPORT CARD

Brainstorm as a class different ways students can show kindness to and encourage others, such as smiling, saying a kind word, eating lunch with a friend, offering some help to someone who is busy, or doing a chore without being asked. Have students keep track of their own good and kind acts by having them draw a picture or place a sticker on a square of Santa's Report Card each time they remember to do a kind act. Invite students to share their report card with their family on Christmas Eve.

MATERIALS
▲ Santa's Report Card (page 31)
▲ crayons or stickers

SANTA'S REPORT CARD

	Sunday	Monday	Tuesday	Wednesday	Thursday	Friday	Saturday
I said something nice to someone.		♥	★	rainbow	cat	★	
I cleaned my room.		☺					rainbow
I did my homework.		☺	★	♥	☺		
I helped mom or dad.		♥		♥			♥
I helped my brother or sister.		♥					★
I was kind to someone.			★	★		♥	
I tried my best.		☺		☺			♥

SANTA HANDPRINTS

Have students paint one hand with red paint and make an upside-down handprint with fingers together and thumb extended on the front of a construction-paper card. After the paint dries, students can paint a white beard on the fingers and a Santa hat on the thumb and top of the palm. Have students glue on sequin eyes and a cotton ball on the tip of the thumb. Invite students to write inside the card *My little hand, round and fat, turned into Santa, just like that!*

MATERIALS
▲ white construction paper
▲ red and white paint/paintbrushes
▲ glue
▲ sequins
▲ cotton balls

My little hand,
Round and fat,
Turned into Santa,
Just like that!

Conner

SHAPE SANTA

Invite students to create a Santa from geometric shapes. Have students cut out a large red construction-paper triangle for Santa's body and a small red triangle for his hat. Invite students to cut red rectangles for his arms and white ovals for his mittens. Students can cut out a pink circle for his face and a white triangle for his beard. Have students cut out black rectangles for his legs and feet. Invite students to arrange their shapes on green construction paper and glue on the pieces. Students can glue a cotton ball to the top of the hat and add sequins for Santa's eyes and nose.

Kobe

DRESS-UP SANTA

Divide the class into three or four groups. Have each group decide on one person from their group to decorate like Santa. Give each group one or two rolls of bathroom tissue paper, a package of red tissue paper, some cotton balls, and a roll of cellophane tape. Invite the groups to use the supplies to decorate their "Santa" for about five minutes. Then ask another teacher to choose the best-looking Santa. Take photographs of all the Santas with the "elves" and display the photos in the classroom.

CINNAMON STICK SANTAS

Invite students to blend red and white paint to create pink and paint a Santa face on a cinnamon stick. Have students paint a red hat above the face and a white beard below. When the paint dries, invite students to use black fine-tip permanent markers to add two dot eyes. Help students glue on a pin backing.

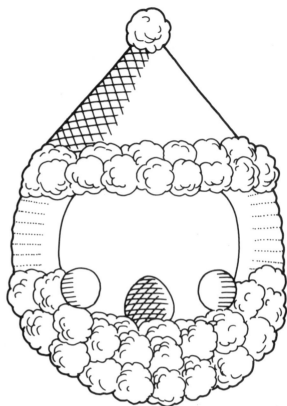

MATERIALS

▲ paper plates
▲ red and pink construction paper
▲ cotton balls
▲ scissors
▲ glue
▲ stapler

SANTA CLAUS MASK

Help students cut the center out of a paper plate and save the rim. Have students cut out a red triangle hat from construction paper and glue it to the top of the rim. Invite students to glue on a cotton ball at the point of the hat and a strip of cotton balls along the bottom of the hat and along the bottom of the plate to make Santa's beard. Students can cut out and glue on pink cheeks and a red nose. Help students staple the end of a red construction-paper strip to each side of the back of the mask so the strip holds the mask in place. Staple the masks to fit each student's head. Invite students to sing "Jolly Old Santa" while they wear their masks.

Jolly Old Santa

(to the tune of "I'm a Little Teapot")

I'm a little Santa, jolly and fat.
Here is my beard and here is my hat.
On Christmas Eve, I'm going to pack
Lots of goodies in my sack!

MATERIALS

▲ potatoes
▲ materials from home (art supplies such as cotton balls, fabric scraps, markers, glue)

HOME ACTIVITY

POTATO CLAUS

Invite students to decorate a potato to look like Santa Claus. Encourage students to work with their families and be creative as they use materials at home such as cotton balls, fabric scraps, or markers to create a funny Potato Claus. Have students return their decorated potatoes to school and share them with the class on a designated day.

SANTA MOBILE

SANTA'S REPORT CARD

Sunday	Monday	Tuesday	Wednesday	Thursday	Friday	Saturday
I said some-thing nice to someone.						
I cleaned my room.						
I did my homework.						
I helped my mom or dad.						
I helped my brother or sister.						
I was kind to someone.						
I tried my best.						

December © 1998 Creative Teaching Press

SNOWMEN

December is a time for building snowmen in many areas. Celebrate the joy snowmen bring with these "cool" activities!

LITERATURE LINKS

HANDY DANDY SNOWMAN BULLETIN BOARD

Cut a large snowman shape from light-blue butcher paper and attach it to a bulletin board. Invite students to dip their hand in white paint and press their handprint to the snowman shape so the snowman is covered with handprints. Invite students to press their thumbs into the paint to make thumbprint snowflakes on the background. When the paint dries, attach a black construction-paper hat, an orange nose, twig arms, button eyes, a pom-pom mouth, and a felt scarf. Hang student work on the bulletin board titled *Room __'s Handy Dandy Snowman.*

MATERIALS
▲ light-blue butcher paper
▲ white paint
▲ paper plates
▲ black and orange construction paper
▲ twigs
▲ buttons
▲ pom-poms
▲ felt

"FOLLOW DIRECTIONS" SNOWMEN

Tell students they will draw a snowman according to the directions or "secret code" you give them. Tell girl students to draw their snowman with two circles and boy students to draw their snowman with three circles. Tell blue-eyed students to draw circles for eyes, brown-eyed students to draw circles with dots in the center, and green-eyed students to draw triangle eyes. Have students who get a ride to school draw a carrot nose and students who walk to school draw a pig nose. Ask students who wear glasses to draw a closed-mouth smile and students who do not wear glasses to draw an open-mouth smile. Have all students draw a scarf and make the number of fringes equal their age. Have students draw an open-circle "button" for each sister they have and a closed-circle button for each brother. Have dark-haired students draw a top hat and light-haired students draw a ski cap. Add any other directions for your students to help them draw snowmen that reveal something about themselves.

SPARKLY SNOWMEN

Copy the Snowman pattern on light-blue construction paper, and have students cut out the patterns. Pour white paint onto paper plates and add coarse salt to give it a sparkly texture. Invite students to paint their snowman with the textured paint. As the paint dries, take a walk outdoors and invite students to hunt for twigs. Have students glue twig arms, button eyes, an orange paper carrot nose, a felt scarf, a black construction-paper hat, and buttons on their snow-man. Display the snowmen in the classroom.

RACE THE SNOWMAN MATH GAME

MATERIALS
▲ 4" x 18" (10 cm x 46 cm) construction-paper strips
▲ snowman die cuts or stickers
▲ dice
▲ cotton balls

To make the game, draw a line down the center of a construction-paper strip, glue a snowman to one end, and label the left side of the strip *A* and the right side of the strip *B*. Give one game strip to every two players. Players take turns rolling the dice. Have players add the numbers on the dice and line up an equal amount of cotton balls on their side of the strip. The object of the game is for students to line up the cotton balls along their side and reach the snowman before their partner does. The first player to have cotton balls lined up to the snowman wins. Older players can record the addition problems as they add more cotton balls. For subtraction practice fun, have students take away the cotton balls in the same way.

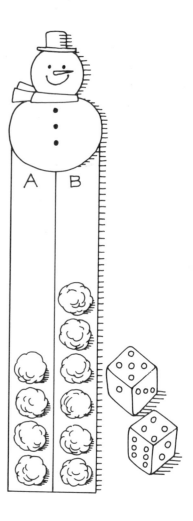

TEAR-ART SNOWMAN

MATERIALS
▲ Snowman reproducible (page 37)
▲ tagboard
▲ scissors
▲ white and black construction paper
▲ art supplies (buttons, fabric scraps, sequins, wiggly eyes)

Trace the Snowman pattern on tagboard and have each student cut out the pattern. Invite students to tear white paper and glue it over the snowman shape. Have students cut out a black construction-paper hat. Invite students to add a fabric scarf, buttons down the front, a sequin mouth, and wiggly eyes. Attach the "Snowman Song" to the back of the snowman. Invite students to sing the song as they hold up their snowmen.

Snowman Song
(to the tune of "Clementine")

I'm a snowman,
A jolly snowman,
Made of three big balls of snow.
We can play in winter weather,
But when the sun comes,
I must go!

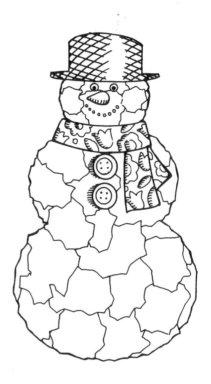

SNOWMAN MATH MANIPULATIVES

Ask students to glue three cotton balls, two eyes, a mouth, and three buttons on index cards to make snowmen. Have students glue a fabric scarf to each snowman's "neck." Instruct students to draw stick arms with brown crayon. Gather the class in a circle with their snowmen. Have a volunteer take a math-fact card and use snowmen to make the equation. Have students count out the corresponding sets of snowmen to match the equation. Recite the equation as a class. Then invite another volunteer to take a card.

MARSHMALLOW SNOWMAN ORNAMENTS

Cut one large marshmallow in half for each student. Have students glue one half marshmallow "head" to one whole marshmallow "body." Invite students to glue a small piece of red felt to the half marshmallow to make the brim of a hat and glue the other half of the marshmallow on the felt to make a hat. Have students draw a face on the head using markers. Invite students to glue four miniature marshmallows to the body to make feet and arms. Have students gather a small piece of green felt together in the center to make a bow tie and pin it to the snowman using a straight pin. Help students poke an ornament hook into the snowman's hat and tie a colorful ribbon to the end for a cute ornament.

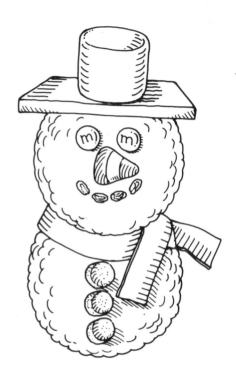

SNOWMAN TREATS

MATERIALS
- ▲ *Snowballs* by Lois Ehlert
- ▲ popcorn balls
- ▲ fruit roll-ups
- ▲ vanilla wafers
- ▲ marshmallows
- ▲ M&Ms
- ▲ candy corn
- ▲ raisins
- ▲ gumdrops

Read aloud *Snowballs.* Make popcorn balls according to the recipe on the back cover of the book. Give each student two small popcorn balls and have them stick them together to make a snowman. Invite students to wrap a fruit roll-up strip around the two balls to make a scarf. Have students stick a vanilla wafer cookie to the top of the snowman and stick a marshmallow on top to make a hat. Invite students to add M&M eyes, a candy corn nose, a raisin mouth, and gumdrop buttons for a delectable snowman treat!

ORDINAL SNOWMEN

MATERIALS
- ▲ long white construction-paper strips
- ▲ crayons or markers

Teach following directions and ordinal numbers with this fun activity. Have students fold a long construction-paper strip accordion-style to make ten sections and draw ten simple snowmen, one in each section. Give oral directions for decorating each snowman, such as *Draw mouse ears on the fourth snowman* and *Draw sunglasses on the sixth snowman.*

COOL STUFF SNOWMEN

HOME ACTIVITY

MATERIALS
- ▲ *Snowballs* by Lois Ehlert
- ▲ Snowman pattern (page 37)
- ▲ scissors
- ▲ white construction paper
- ▲ family letter (page 38)
- ▲ paper sack

Read aloud and discuss *Snowballs.* Trace and cut out the Snowman pattern on white construction paper. Place the snowman and a copy of the family letter in a paper sack labeled *Good Stuff.* Invite students to make their own cool snowmen at home with their family. Tell students they can use any "good stuff" to create their snowman. Invite students to bring their extra "good stuff" to school in the sack. Invite students to share their snowman with the class. Then have students share their good stuff with other students so they can make another snowman. Have students glue the snowmen on construction paper, and then bind into a class big book. As a class, write text to match the snowmen.

HANUKKAH

Hanukkah commemorates a rebellion by Jews against the Syrians more than 2,000 years ago. The tiny amount of oil found in the central temple in Jerusalem after it was destroyed miraculously fueled the Eternal Light for eight days. Hanukkah is celebrated for eight days, beginning on the 25th day of the Hebrew month of Kislev (between November and December).

LITERATURE LINKS

All about Hanukkah
by Judyth Groner

All the Lights in the Night
by Arthur A. Levine

The Chanukah Guest
by Eric A. Kimmel

Hanukkah
by Miriam Chaikin

Latkes and Applesauce
by Fran Manushkin

Malke's Secret Recipe
by David A. Adler

One Yellow Daffodil
by David A. Adler

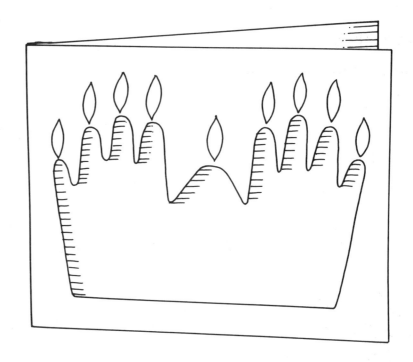

HANUKKAH HANDS

Blue and white are the colors of Israel's flag and are also symbolic of Hanukkah. Invite students to place their hands on blue construction paper side by side so their thumbs overlap to create the shamash candle (which is used to light all the other candles). Ask students to have a partner trace their hands. Have students cut out their handprints in one piece to create a menorah and glue it to folded white construction paper to make a card. Have students use a gold marker to add flames above the candles. Invite students to write a Hanukkah message inside the card.

MATERIALS
- ▲ blue and white construction paper
- ▲ scissors
- ▲ glue
- ▲ gold markers

SPIN THE DREIDEL

MATERIALS
- ▲ Dreidel reproducible (page 43)
- ▲ scissors
- ▲ glue
- ▲ pencil
- ▲ manipulatives (beans, chocolates, or peanuts)

The four sides of a dreidel are decorated with the first four letters from the Hebrew phrase *Nes gadol hayah sham,* which means *A great miracle happened here.* Dreidels are reminders of the miracle of the lamp. Have students cut out the dreidel from the reproducible, fold it on the dotted lines, and glue the tabs. Have students push a pencil through the top of the dreidel. To play, everyone begins with an equal amount of beans, chocolates, or peanuts. Before each round, have students place one manipulative in the center of the playing area. Players spin in turn and follow directions based on the letter that is faceup when the dreidel stops (see the key below). Players continue until one player has all the manipulatives.

nun   = Take nothing from the pot.
gimmel = Take the whole pot.
hay   = Take half the pot.
shin   = Add two items to the pot.

DREIDEL CARD

MATERIALS
- ▲ envelopes
- ▲ glue
- ▲ construction paper
- ▲ crayons or markers

Have each student open the flaps to two same-size envelopes. Have students glue the flaps and sides together (with the backs of the envelopes facing each other) and leave the bottom of the envelopes unglued to make a pouch inside. Have students cut a construction-paper handle that is long enough to slide all the way into the pocket to the point of the envelope, leaving a few inches sticking out at the other end. Invite students to write a Hanukkah message on the part of the handle that will be hidden and slide the handle into the dreidel pocket. Have students decorate the dreidel card and give it to a friend. Sing "The Little Dreidel" song with your class.

The Little Dreidel
(to the tune of "I'm a Little Teapot")

I'm a little dreidel, spinning round.
You can pick me up if I fall down.
I'm just a little game that's fun to play.
I wish Hanukkah were every day!

MY MENORAH

MATERIALS

▲ Menorah reproducible (page 44)

▲ light blue paper

▲ scissors

▲ scrap paper

▲ glue

▲ straws

▲ orange yarn

Have students trace the Menorah reproducible on folded blue construction paper and cut it out. Have students copy the "Hanukkah" song on scrap paper and glue it to the back of the menorah. Invite students to cut straws into equal lengths (except one longer one for the center) and glue them on the menorah to make candles. Have students glue a piece of orange yarn on a candle each day of Hanukkah to represent the lighting of the candles.

Hanukkah

(to the tune of "Three Blind Mice")

Hanukkah, Hanukkah,
Eight special nights, nine special lights,
We light one candle for every night
To remember the miracle that was a great sight
When the oil lasted eight days and nights.
On Hanukkah.

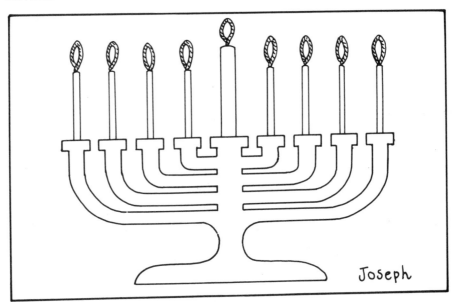

Joseph

STAR OF DAVID

MATERIALS

▲ Star of David pattern (page 45)

▲ cardboard

▲ hole punch

▲ glue

▲ macaroni

▲ blue tempera paint/paintbrushes

▲ silver glitter spray paint

▲ blue ribbon

The Star of David is the universal symbol of Judaism. Cut out and trace the Star of David pattern onto cardboard for each student. Have students hole-punch one point in the star and glue macaroni to fill both sides of the star. When the glue dries, have students paint both sides of the star blue. Spray the dried stars with silver glitter spray paint. Hang the stars from blue ribbon around the classroom.

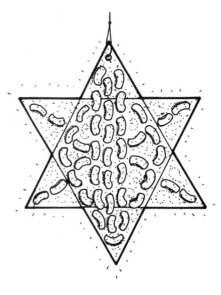

MENORAH POP-OUT CARD

Invite students to fold blue construction paper in half to make a card. Students can make a large "pop-out spring" from two yellow construction-paper strips; they apply glue to the end of one strip and lay the other strip on the glue at a right angle to the first. Then students fold and overlap strips until all the paper is folded into a chain. Have students glue one end of the spring to the side of the fold line inside the card and apply glue to the other end of the spring. Have students press the card closed while the glue dries. Invite students to cut and glue eight tiny construction-paper candles to the sides and top of the spring. Have students draw one long candle in the center of the fold to be the shamash candle. Invite students to decorate the front of the card and write a Hanukkah greeting.

LATKES

Latke is a Russian word for *flat cake.* Latkes, or potato pancakes, are served for this holiday around the world because Jews want to serve a dish cooked in oil to symbolize the miracle of Hanukkah. During the eight days of Hanukkah, latkes are eaten daily. Make the following recipe as a class to enjoy this typical Hanukkah treat.

1. Peel potatoes and cut into chunks. Peel and cut onion into chunks.
2. Shred potatoes and onion in a food processor. Remove and squeeze out excess water.
3. Add remaining ingredients to potato mixture and stir well. If mixture is too watery, add more matzoh meal.
4. Heat oil in an electric skillet. When oil is hot, drop a spoonful of mixture into the pan.
5. Fry over medium heat until brown on each side.
6. Remove latkes and dry on paper towels to remove excess oil. Fry the remaining mixture. Serve latkes with applesauce or sour cream.

DREIDEL

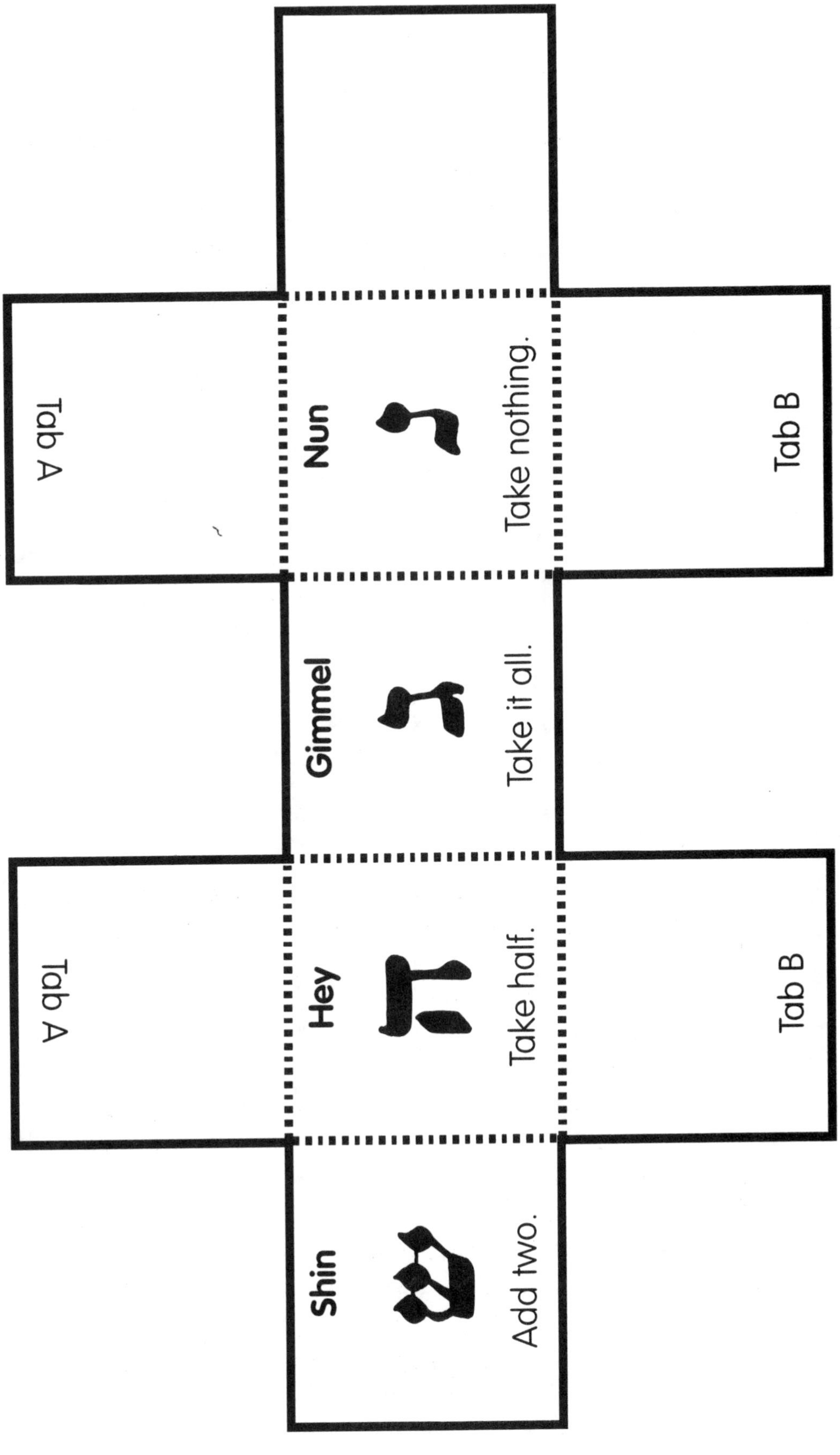

Tab A

Nun

Take nothing.

Tab B

Gimmel

Take it all.

Tab A

Hey

Take half.

Tab B

Shin

Add two.

MENORAH

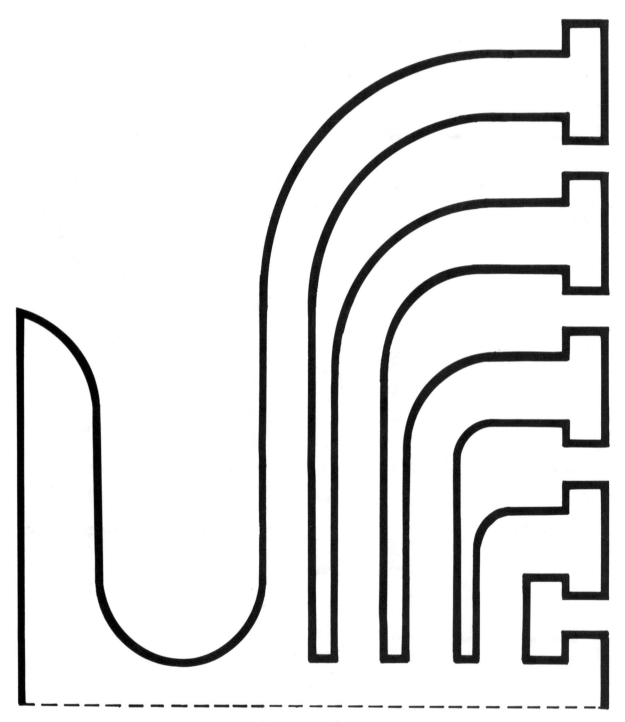

Place on fold.

December © 1998 Creative Teaching Press

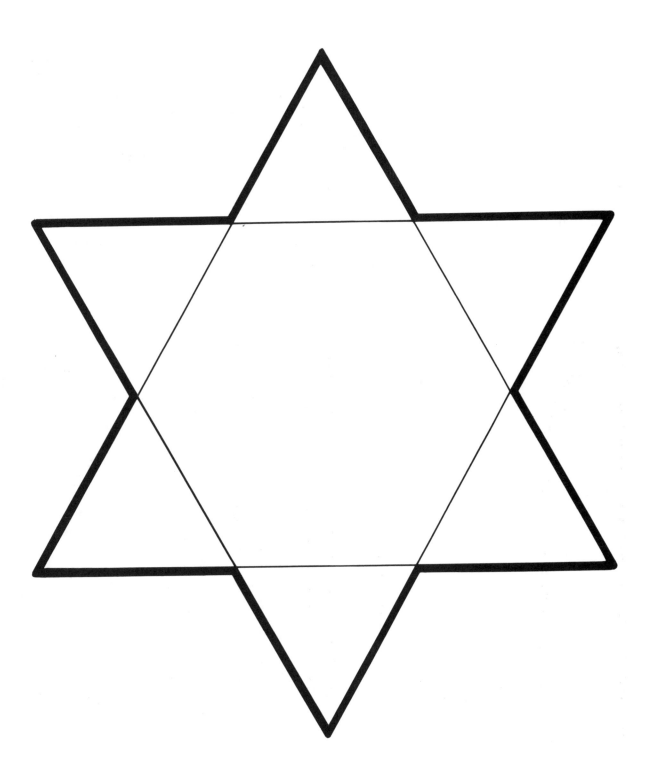

STAR OF DAVID

December © 1998 Creative Teaching Press

MARVELOUS MITTENS DAY

December 3

As the cold December winds blow, it's time in many parts of the country to wear mittens to keep those little fingers toasty. Mittens can help teach math, tell a story, or be used in matching activities. Try the following activities and have fun with some "mittens-on" learning!

LITERATURE LINKS

A Bad Start for Santa Claus
by Sarah Hayes

Caps, Hats, Socks, Mittens: A Book about the Four Seasons
by Louise Borden

Junie B. Jones Is Not a Crook
by Barbara Park

The Mitten by Alvin Tresselt

The Mitten by Jan Brett

The Mitten Tree
by Candice Christiansen

Runaway Mittens
by Jean Rogers

Three Little Kittens
by Paul Galdone

Cool Contractions

can't — can | not
didn't — did | not
she'll — she | will
you're — you | are
won't — will | not
he'd — he | would

MITTEN CONTRACTIONS

Invite students to write on the Mittens pattern two words that can be made into a contraction, one word per mitten. Invite students to write on a construction-paper circle "snowball" the contraction that is made from the two words. Have students hole-punch the bottom of each mitten and tie a piece of yarn or string to connect the pair. Invite students to color a matching pattern on each pair of mittens. Display mittens and snowballs on a bulletin board titled *Cool Contractions*.

MATERIALS

▲ Mittens pattern (page 48)
▲ white construction-paper circles
▲ scissors
▲ hole punch
▲ yarn
▲ crayons or markers

MITTEN MATH

Have students work with a partner to draw a line around each other's hand (fingers together, thumbs extended) to make a mitten. Then have students write a math problem on one side of the mitten and the answer on the other side. Store the mittens in a winter cap. During math time, have students pull a mitten from the cap and solve the problem. Students can check their work by looking at the back side.

MATERIALS

▲ construction paper
▲ scissors
▲ winter cap

MITTEN-MAKING

MATERIALS

▲ Mittens pattern (page 48)
▲ construction paper
▲ hole punch
▲ 36" (1 m) pieces of yarn
▲ tissue

Have each student cut out two sets of mittens and arrange them so they look like a pair of mittens. Help students hole-punch all along the sides and top of the mittens. Have students thread yarn through the bottom hole near the thumb and tie a knot. Invite students to thread the yarn up and down through the holes all the way around the mitten and make another knot to tie off the yarn. Let the yarn hang down. Have students repeat with the other mitten and then tie the two mittens together. Invite students to carefully stuff each mitten with tissue. Have students write a winter word on each mitten. Hang the mittens on a bulletin board titled *Need a hand with winter words? Try these on for size!*

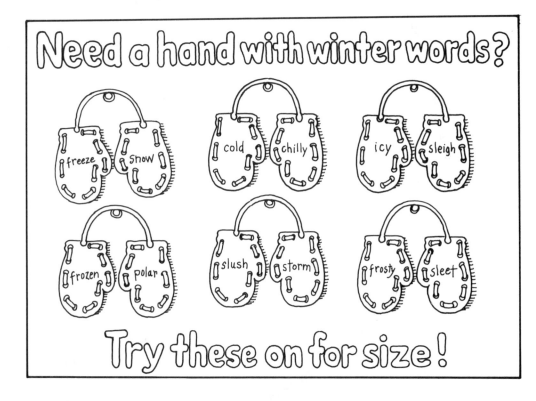

WALT DISNEY DAY

December 5

Walt Disney was born on this day in 1901. He created such cartoon film characters as Mickey Mouse and Donald Duck. The first full-length cartoon film ever made was Disney's *Snow White and the Seven Dwarfs*. He achieved one of his greatest successes when he opened Disneyland in 1955. Your students may find their dreams come true with these imaginative activities.

LITERATURE LINKS

The Big Date by Walt Disney

The Man behind the Magic: The Story of Walt Disney Katherine Greene et al.

The Story of Walt Disney: Maker of Magical Worlds by Bernice Selden

Walt Disney's Treasury of Children's Classics edited by Darlene Geis

MICKEY MOUSE CUPCAKES

Mickey Mouse starred in Walt Disney's first animated cartoon, *Steamboat Willie*. Celebrate this much-loved character with Mickey Mouse cupcakes. In advance, bake cupcakes, one per student. Invite students to frost their cupcake. Then, students can add sandwich-cookie ears, M&M eyes, a chocolate-kiss nose, and red hots for a smile.

MATERIALS
▲ cupcakes
▲ frosting
▲ plastic knives
▲ sandwich cookies
▲ M&Ms
▲ chocolate kisses
▲ red hots

TINKERBELL READING WANDS

Have students dip a straw or chopstick in glue and then glitter to make reading wands. When the glue dries, invite students to wrap ribbon around the wands and attach a construction-paper star to one end. Have students use the wands for pointing to words while reading.

THE HAPPIEST PLACE ON EARTH

HOME ACTIVITY

Walt Disney had a great imagination. He imagined the happiest place on earth and created Disneyland. Invite students to create their idea of the happiest place on earth. Invite students to use art supplies or other materials from home to create their idea of the happiest place and share it with the class.

COTTON BALL DAY

December 8

Eli Whitney, born on this date in 1765, invented the cotton gin, which helped remove cotton seeds from the cotton fiber more quickly and inexpensively than by hand. Invite students to use cotton balls for math and art, and as a history lesson. And since cotton balls look like snow, they are the perfect December subject!

LITERATURE LINKS

The Cotton in Your T-Shirt
by Aline Riquier

From Cotton to Pants
by Ali Mitgutsch

From Plant to Blue Jeans: A Photo Essay
by Arthur John L'Hommedieu

Joseph and the Cottonseed
by Belinda and John Taylor

Working Cotton
by Sherley Anne Williams

COTTON DOT PAINTING

Have students attach clothespins to cotton balls. Invite students to dip a cotton ball into paint and dab it on construction paper to create a winter wonderland scene. (The cotton gives a soft look.) Invite students to glue extra cotton balls to the art project. Cotton balls can be used as clouds, snowmen, igloos, or snow on mountains.

MATERIALS
▲ cotton balls
▲ clothespins
▲ paint or pastels
▲ construction paper
▲ glue

MATERIALS

▲ cotton balls
▲ jar
▲ glue
▲ construction paper
▲ crayons or paint/paint-brushes

COTTON BALL ESTIMATION

Fill a jar with cotton balls. Write inside the jar lid the number of cotton balls in the jar. Invite students to pass the jar and estimate how many cotton balls are inside. Ask volunteers to count the cotton balls. Have another volunteer tally the number on the chalkboard.

MATERIALS

▲ blindfold
▲ cotton balls
▲ spatula
▲ paper plate

CAN YOU FEEL IT? GAME

Have students sit in a circle on the floor with cotton balls in the center. Ask students to estimate how many cotton balls they think they can scoop up in one minute while blindfolded. Blindfold a student and have the student hold a paper plate on his or her head with one hand and hold a spatula in the other hand. Time students for one minute each as they try to scoop cotton balls onto the plate on their head. Have students determine the difference between how many cotton balls they picked up and how many cotton balls they estimated they would pick up.

DECK THE HALLS DAY

December is the perfect time to get your students involved in decorating the classroom. Have a jolly good time decorating with the fa-la-la-la-la-llowing activities.

The Giving Tree

LITERATURE LINKS

Deck the Halls
by Jennie Williams

*Deck the Halls:
An Old Welsh Carol*
by Iris Van Rynbach

*Deck the Halls:
A Musical Board Book*
by Ruth Hill

*Jingle Jokes: Christmas Riddles
to Deck the Ha Ha Halls*
by Katy Hall and
Lisa Eisenberg

O CHRISTMAS TREE BULLETIN BOARD

Cut holiday wrapping paper into a large triangular tree shape. Staple the wrapping paper to a bulletin board. Invite students to trace their hands on green paper, cut the tracings out, and write a holiday wish on the palms (the fingers should point downward). Have students use a pencil to curl the fingers upward and then add glitter glue to the fingertips. Help students staple their handprints to the wrapping paper, with the fingers pointing downward, in rows to form a tree shape. Include a few gift-wrapped packages around the tree. Place a star at the top of the tree. Title the bulletin board *The Giving Tree.*

MATERIALS
▲ holiday wrapping paper
▲ green construction paper
▲ stapler
▲ scissors
▲ pencils
▲ glitter glue
▲ construction-paper star

BOUGHS OF POINSETTIAS

The poinsettia is a wildflower native to Mexico. Legend tells of an old Mexican tradition when a manger at church was filled with flowers on Christmas Eve. A small Mexican boy was brokenhearted when he had no flowers to bring. An angel appeared and told the boy to pick a handful of weeds. When the boy placed the weeds in a manger they turned into lovely red star-shaped flowers—poinsettias. Have students place a 2" (5 cm) circle in the center of a red construction-paper circle. Have students fold the circle in half, in half again, in half a third time, and unfold. Ask them to cut on all the fold lines from the outside to the center circle to make petals. Have students fold the ends of each petal to form a point and glue the ends together. Invite students to push up the points to make the flower three-dimensional. Have students hole-punch yellow construction paper to make dots and glue them to the center of the flower. Then deck the halls with boughs of poinsettias!

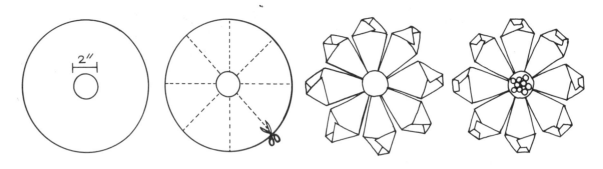

MATERIALS

▲ popcorn

▲ big, dull needles

▲ thread

POPCORN GARLANDS

Pop a batch of popcorn. Invite students to use a sewing needle and doubled thread to string popped kernels. Have them drape the finished garlands around the classroom and then take them home to decorate an outside door or tree. Birds will love the special treat.

MATERIALS

▲ black construction
paper

▲ scissors

▲ colored tissue paper

STAINED GLASS BUILDINGS

Invite students to draw houses and interesting buildings on black construction paper. Help students cut out the windows or doors. Invite students to glue different-colored tissue paper to the back of the buildings or houses to create a stained-glass effect. Tape the completed papers to a window so light shines through the "stained glass."

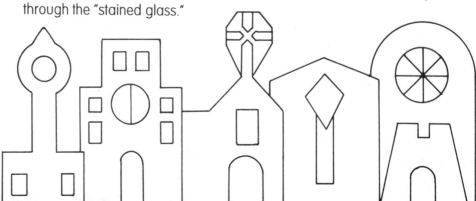

COOKIE DAY

December is the perfect time for baking holiday cookies with kids. Try the following activities— they're yummy!

LITERATURE LINKS

The Biggest Cookie in the World
by Linda Hayward

The Case of the Missing Cookies
by Denise Lewis Patrick

Cookie Count: A Tasty Pop-Up
by Robert Sabuda

Cookie Fun
by Judy Bastyra

Cookie Shapes
by John Fosberg

A Cow, a Bee, a Cookie, and Me
by Meredith Hooper

The Doorbell Rang
by Pat Hutchins

If You Give a Mouse a Cookie
by Laura J. Numeroff

Who Took the Cookies from the Cookie Jar?
CTP Learn to Read Series

GINGERBREAD COOKIES

Melt butter. Put sugar and molasses in a large bowl and pour in butter. Stir remaining ingredients together. Gradually add dry ingredients to wet ingredients. Knead dough until well-blended. Roll dough to ¼" (1 cm) thickness directly on a lightly greased cookie sheet. Invite students to cut the dough with gingerbread-people cookie cutters. Bake in a 350°F (175°C) oven for 8–10 minutes. Remove from the oven and cool. Invite students to decorate cooled cookies with frosting and small candies.

MATERIALS
- ▲ 1 cup (250 ml) butter
- ▲ 1 cup (250 ml) sugar
- ▲ 1 cup (250 ml) molasses
- ▲ 5 cups (1250 ml) flour
- ▲ 1 teaspoon (5 ml) baking soda
- ▲ 1 teaspoon (5 ml) salt
- ▲ 1 teaspoon (5 ml) nutmeg
- ▲ 1 tablespoon ginger
- ▲ rolling pin
- ▲ greased cookie sheets
- ▲ gingerbread-people cookie cutters
- ▲ frosting in tubes
- ▲ small candies

CANDY CANE COOKIES

MATERIALS
- ▲ 1 ¼ cups (300 ml) butter
- ▲ 1 cup (250 ml) powdered sugar
- ▲ 1 egg
- ▲ 1 teaspoon (5 ml) vanilla
- ▲ ½ teaspoon (2 ml) almond extract
- ▲ 3 ½ cups (800 ml) flour
- ▲ 1 teaspoon (5 ml) salt
- ▲ red food coloring
- ▲ cookie sheets

Cream butter, add sugar, and mix well. Add egg, vanilla, and almond extract. Add flour and salt and mix well. Divide the dough in half and tint one part red. To make canes, have students roll 1 teaspoon of red dough into a 4" (10 cm) strip. Have students twist red and white strips of dough together lightly. Place the twists on an ungreased cookie sheet and curve the tip to form the handle. Bake at 350° (175° C) for 10–12 minutes.

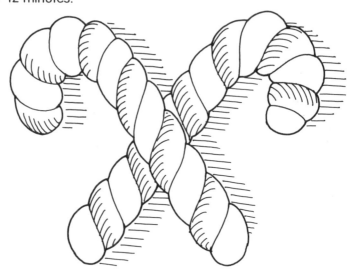

REINDEER COOKIES CLASS BOOK

MATERIALS
- ▲ crayons or markers
- ▲ bookbinding materials

Ask students to think of special cookies for Santa's reindeer. Invite students to draw their imaginary cookie and write a description of it in the sentence frame *Rudolph gets some cookies this year. _____ cookies bring him cheer.* Bind pages together in a class book called *Cookies for Rudolph.*

HOT CHOCOLATE DAY

There's nothing like a hot cup of cocoa on a chilly December day. Warm up your class with these toasty activities.

I feel warm and toasty when I snuggle under my quilt with my teddy bear.

LITERATURE LINKS

Chocolate Fever
by Robert Kimmel Smith

"Chocolate Rhyme" from *Tortillitas Para Mama* selected by Margot Griego et al.

Harold and Chester in Hot Fudge
by James Howe

Making Your Own Gourmet Chocolate Drinks: Hot Drinks, Cold Drinks, Sodas, Floats, Shakes, and More!
by Mathew Tekulsky

Shoogies Marshmallow Rain
by Pam Davidson

WARM AND TOASTY FEELINGS

Cut from construction paper a large class book shaped like a cup of hot cocoa. Ask students to write on a mug-shaped page what makes them feel warm and toasty. For example, *I feel warm and toasty when my daddy hugs me* or *I feel warm and toasty when I read a good book by the fire.* Then have students decorate each page with sponge-painted designs. Invite students to sing "Hot Chocolate."

Hot Chocolate
(to the tune of "Are You Sleeping?")

Nice hot chocolate,
Nice hot chocolate,
Yum, yum, yum,
Yum, yum, yum!
Marshmallows are floating.
Whipped cream is melting.
Yum, yum, yum,
In my tum!

MATERIALS
▲ large construction paper
▲ scissors
▲ sponges
▲ tempera paint
▲ bookbinding materials

HOT CHOCOLATE VOCABULARY GAME

MATERIALS
- ▲ index cards
- ▲ coffee mugs
- ▲ dice
- ▲ paper

Brainstorm a list of words related to hot chocolate, such as *sweet, warm, smooth, yummy, toasty, marshmallows, cocoa, drink, mug, steamy, stir,* and *melt.* Group students, and for each group, print a different word on each of two sets of six index cards and number the backs from 1 to 6. Place one set of cards and a die in a mug and another set of cards and a die in another mug for each group. Have groups place each set of words facedown. Invite one group member to roll the dice, flip over a card from each pile that matches the number rolled, and say or write a sentence using both of the words. Ask group members to take turns until everyone has created a sentence. Challenge groups to write or tell a story using all of the sentences from their group and share it with the class.

INSTANT SPICE MOCHA

MATERIALS
- ▲ jars with lids
- ▲ holiday or plaid fabric
- ▲ ribbon
- ▲ glue
- ▲ pinking shears
- ▲ instant hot cocoa mix
- ▲ instant coffee powder
- ▲ sugar
- ▲ dried non-dairy creamer
- ▲ ground cinnamon
- ▲ nutmeg
- ▲ construction paper

Ask students to bring in a jar with a lid. Use pinking shears to cut circles slightly larger than the jar lids from holiday or plaid fabric. Have students glue the fabric circles to the jar lids and tie on a ribbon to secure them. Invite students to decorate the jar with paint or permanent markers. Have each student fill their jar with three parts instant hot cocoa mix, three parts instant coffee powder, two and a half parts non-dairy creamer, one part sugar, and a dash of cinnamon and nutmeg. Have students make a gift tag from construction paper and tie it around the lid with a ribbon. Students can give the instant spice mocha as a gift to a family member.

MERRY MUSIC DAY

December 16

Ludwig van Beethoven, born on this date in 1770, is regarded by many as one of the greatest composers of all time. Despite a hearing loss that ended in total deafness, Beethoven composed and conducted throughout his life. His works include "Moonlight Sonata," Symphony no. 9, and Symphony no. 5.

LITERATURE LINKS

Beethoven by Ann Rachlin

Beethoven Lives Upstairs by Barbara Nichol

Beethoven's Cat by Elisabet McHugh

Her Piano Sang by Barbara Allman

Ludwig van Beethoven: Musical Pioneer by Carol Greene

Ludwig Van Beethoven by Mike Venezia

Meet the Orchestra by Ann Hayes

CHECK OUT THAT HAIR!

Read aloud and discuss a book about Beethoven. Beethoven was known for his wild hair. Invite students to draw a self-portrait on the Beethoven reproducible. Then have students glue white and gray yarn to the head for a "wild" Beethoven masterpiece. Have students write or dictate in a speech bubble something they learned about Beethoven and attach it above their artwork. Hang the portraits on a bulletin board titled *I, Beethoven . . . .*

MATERIALS
▲ book about Beethoven
▲ Beethoven reproducible (page 61)
▲ crayons or markers
▲ white and gray yarn
▲ speech bubbles

PIANO PLAYER

MATERIALS

▲ Piano pattern (page 62)

▲ black and white construction paper

▲ scissors

▲ glue

Have each student trace the piano and keyboard patterns on construction paper and cut them out. Ask students to glue the keyboard behind the black piano. Invite students to color the black piano keys in the pattern two, three, two, three, two, three. Have students write on their piano *The piano has 88 keys: 52 white keys and 36 black keys.* Hang the pianos from the ceiling.

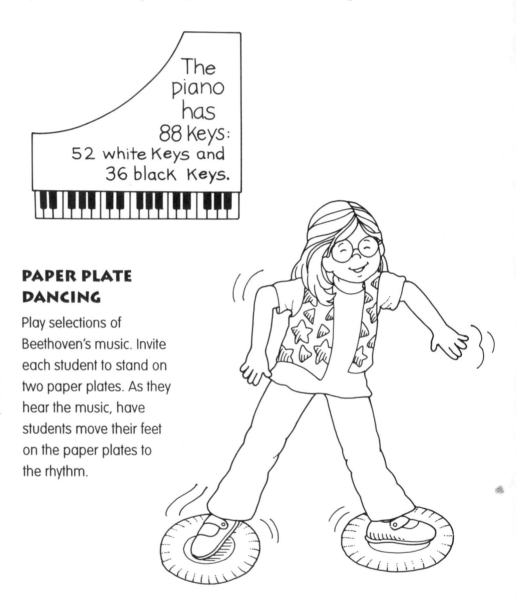

PAPER PLATE DANCING

MATERIALS

▲ paper plates

▲ selections of Beethoven's music

▲ audiocassette or CD player

Play selections of Beethoven's music. Invite each student to stand on two paper plates. As they hear the music, have students move their feet on the paper plates to the rhythm.

HEAR THE RHYTHM

MATERIALS

▲ selections of Beethoven's music

▲ audio cassette or CD player with adjustable bass and speakers

Tell students that Beethoven became deaf later in his life, yet he still played and wrote music. Show students how they can "feel" music the way Beethoven may have "listened" to it. Play Beethoven's music and turn up the bass. Put the speakers on the floor and have students place their hands on the floor to feel the beat.

BEETHOVEN

PIANO

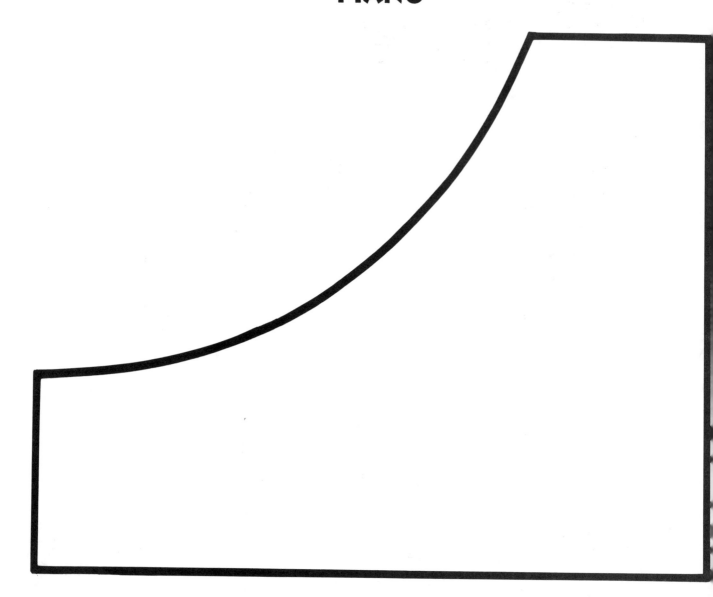

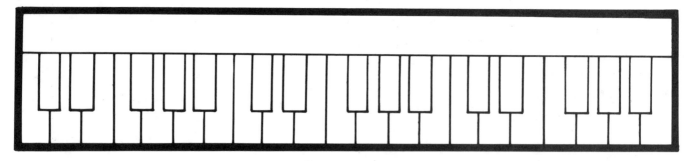

December © 1998 Creative Teaching Press

MAKE-A-GIFT DAY

'Tis the season to give gifts! Invite students to experience the joy of giving with these darling gift ideas.

LITERATURE LINKS

The Animals' Gift
by Szabolcs De Vajay

The Best Gift for Mom
by Lee Klein

The Extraordinary Gift
by Florence Langlois

The Gift of the Magi
by O. Henry

The Giving Tree
by Shel Silverstein

The Hummingbird's Gift
by Stefan Czernecki

Scrap Savers: One Hundred One Great Little Gifts
by Sandra L. Foose

ADORABLE ANGELS

Cut construction-paper circles the same size as the doilies. Have students glue a doily over a construction-paper circle, cut a slit from the outer circle to the center, and form the circle into a cone. Use a hot glue gun to glue a wooden ball to the point of the cone. Have each student cut one doily in half. Have students cut one piece in half again to make two arms. Help students fold the two arms in half and glue them in place. Instruct students to gather the other doily half in the center and secure it with a gold pipe cleaner to make wings. Glue the wings in place. Have students add corn silk "hair" to the wooden ball and wrap a halo of gold wire stars on the hair. Invite students to give their angel to a special family member.

MATERIALS
- ▲ construction paper
- ▲ scissors
- ▲ doilies
- ▲ hot glue gun
- ▲ wooden balls
- ▲ corn silk
- ▲ gold pipe cleaners
- ▲ gold wire stars

HANDPRINT WREATHS

MATERIALS
- ▲ 10" (25.5 cm) muslin squares
- ▲ pinking shears
- ▲ green and red paint/paintbrushes
- ▲ pencil
- ▲ glue
- ▲ 1" x 10" (2.5 cm x 25.5 cm) tagboard strips
- ▲ hole punch
- ▲ plaid ribbon
- ▲ gold paint pen

Cut with pinking shears one muslin square for each student. Lightly trace a circle in the center of the square with pencil. Invite students to paint one hand with green paint and press it onto the muslin, fingers pointed outward, around the edges of the "wreath." Students will need to repaint their hand to keep the color dark as they make more handprints to complete the circle. Let the paint dry. Invite students to paint their thumb red and dot it around the wreath to make berries. Invite students to glue the top edge of the muslin to a tagboard strip. Punch holes in the center of the strip, and invite students to tie a plaid bow to the top. Write each student's name and the date using a gold paint pen.

"I'M AN ANGEL" ORNAMENTS

MATERIALS
- ▲ camera/film
- ▲ Angel reproducible (page 67)
- ▲ doilies
- ▲ glue
- ▲ gold pipe cleaners
- ▲ ornament hooks

Take a photograph of each student. Cut the photographs to fit over the angel face on the reproducible. Have students decorate the angel and then glue their photograph to the face. Ask students to cut out the angel and glue it to a doily. Invite students to write on the back of the doily a holiday greeting and the year. Have students poke an ornament hook though the doily and give it as a present.

WREATH FRAMES

For each student cut a circle out of a green craft foam. Then cut a hole in the center of each circle so a photograph can be glued to the back and show through. Have each student glue old puzzle pieces to the green circle, overlapping the pieces. When students finish, invite them to drizzle glue over the puzzle pieces and sprinkle glitter on the "wreath." Help students make a bow using glitter pipe cleaners and glue the bow to the top of the wreath. Glue student photographs behind the wreaths so their faces show through the center.

PINE TREE CARDS

Cover the work area with newspaper and have students wear paint smocks. Have students place dark blue construction paper on the newspaper, dip an old toothbrush in white paint, and flick the toothbrush to spray the paint onto the paper. When the paint dries, have students fold the paper like a card and glue a small pine tree branch to the front. Invite students to write a holiday greeting inside the card.

PRINT WRAPPING PAPER

MATERIALS
- ▲ white butcher paper
- ▲ tempera paint
- ▲ paper plates
- ▲ holiday cookie cutters

Cut large sheets of butcher paper (large enough to wrap a student's gift). Pour paint on paper plates. Invite students to dip holiday cookie cutters into the paint and make prints on their paper. When the paint dries, have each student wrap a gift using the paper.

BATIK WRAPPING PAPER

MATERIALS
- ▲ white butcher paper
- ▲ bucket
- ▲ batik or clothing dye
- ▲ paint smocks
- ▲ rubber gloves

Invite students to crumple large sheets of butcher paper and dip them into a bucket of batik or clothing dye. (Be sure students are wearing paint smocks and rubber gloves.) Have students carefully squeeze out the excess water and spread out their paper to dry. The paper will have a beautiful batik pattern that makes a special gift wrap.

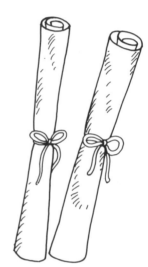

GUESS THE GIFT

MATERIALS
- ▲ box
- ▲ holiday wrapping paper
- ▲ tape

HOME ACTIVITY

Gift-wrap a box with holiday wrapping paper (wrap the box and lid separately). Invite each student to take the box home on a different night. Invite students to place an item from home in the box and write three clues about the item. Have students return the box to school, reveal the clues, and let classmates guess what is in the box.

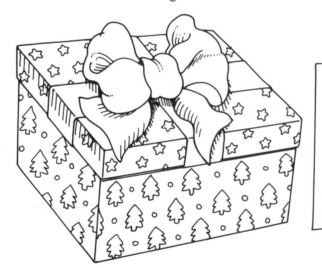

Clues
1. It is something I wear.
2. It keeps the sun off my face.
3. It is worn on my head.

ANGEL

GINGERBREAD DAY

Gingerbread spice is full of everything nice and makes such a festive December holiday treat. Your students will love these "sweet" activities.

Run, Run As Fast As You Can. You Can't Catch Me—

I'm the Gingerbread Man!

LITERATURE LINKS

The Cajun Gingerbread Man by Berthe Amoss

The Gingerbread Boy by Scott Cook

The Gingerbread Boy by Richard Egielski

The Gingerbread Boy by Paul Galdone

The Gingerbread Boy by Hamet Ziefert

The Gingerbread Doll by Susan Tews

The Gingerbread Man by Eric A. Kimmel

The Gingerbread Man: An Old English Folktale by John A. Rowe

GINGERBREAD MURAL

Read aloud and discuss a gingerbread story. Invite students to sponge-paint on butcher paper a path, grass, a sky, and flowers. Have students trace the Gingerbread Man pattern onto brown construction paper and cut it out. Invite students to decorate their gingerbread people with art supplies, such as colored macaroni, glitter, dot paints, holiday wrapping paper, or fabric scraps and glue them on the butcher paper along the path. Title the mural *Run, Run As Fast As You Can. You Can't Catch Me—I'm the Gingerbread Man!*

MATERIALS

▲ a gingerbread story (see Literature Links)
▲ butcher paper
▲ paint
▲ sponges
▲ Gingerbread Man pattern (page 70)
▲ brown construction paper
▲ scissors
▲ art supplies (fabric scraps, ribbon, glitter, dot paints, holiday wrapping paper, sequins, colored macaroni, etc.)
▲ glue

WINTER SOLSTICE

December 21 or 22

The winter solstice marks the beginning of winter and the shortest day of the year in the Northern Hemisphere. At this time the Earth is tilted on its axis so the North Pole is slanted away from the sun, and we get less sunlight. Long ago, people lit fires on the winter solstice to entice the sun to return. Capture the natural splendor of winter with these activities.

LITERATURE LINKS

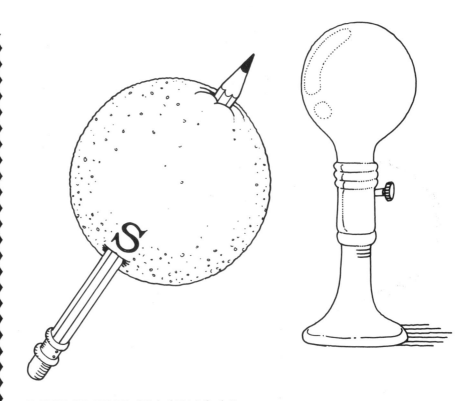

ROUND THE SEASONS GO

Pierce an orange through the center with a pencil to represent the earth on its axis. Use a marker to print N on the top of the orange to show the North Pole and S on the bottom to show the South Pole. Let a lamp with a bare bulb represent the sun. To demonstrate how the seasons change, move the tilted orange in an orbit around the lamp. When there is light shining on the North Pole, it is summer on the top half of the orange (the Northern Hemisphere). The light from the lamp is stronger and makes the top of the orange warmer. When the North Pole becomes shaded, summer is on the bottom half of the orange and it is winter on the top half. The middle of the orange always stays closest to the lamp. Point out that this is the equator, which stays warm year-round.

MATERIALS
▲ orange
▲ pencil
▲ lamp

TROPICAL PICNIC

On the shortest day of the year, invite students to wear summer clothes, such as shorts, Hawaiian shirts, and sunglasses. (Students can bring the clothes and change at school.) Read the story *Moe the Dog in Tropical Paradise.* Invite students to change the classroom into a tropical paradise like Moe did in the story. Provide butcher paper and art supplies for students to create palm trees and a beach scene. Invite students to participate in a "spelling limbo." Ask each student to spell a sight word or former spelling word. If the student is correct, he or she "limbos" under a string held taut. Lower the string for each round. Serve students lemonade in anticipation of summer—it is only six months away!

DESIGNER SNOWSUITS

Read aloud *Thomas' Snowsuit,* the story of a boy who will not wear his snowsuit. Invite each student to design on the Snowsuit reproducible a "designer" snowsuit that Thomas would beg to wear. Have students cut out the snowsuit and glue it to a piece of construction paper. Ask students to write a snowsuit description on the paper. Bind the pages in a class book titled *Thomas's Designer Snowsuits.*

SNOWSUIT

REINDEER DAY

On Dasher, on Dancer, on Prancer, on Vixen, on Comet, on Cupid, on Donner, on Blixen—and don't forget Rudolph! Celebrate Santa's very special helpers with the following activities. Your students will be prancing with excitement!

LITERATURE LINKS

The Christmas Deer
by April Wilson

The Christmas Eve Tradition
by Roderick K. Keitze

Inger's Promise
by Jami Parkison

The Little Reindeer
by Michael Foreman

Olive, the Other Reindeer
by Vivian Walsh

Rudolph the Red-Nosed Reindeer
by Robert L. May

Santa's Ark by Cliff Wright

Where's Prancer? by Syd Hoff

The Wild Christmas Reindeer
by Jan Brett

RUDOLPH HATS

Trace the Rudolph Hat pattern for each student on large folded brown construction paper. Have students fold the top down, fold the sides in, and staple the sides to the top flap as shown. Invite students to cut out eyes and a red nose from construction paper and glue them on the hat. Help students tie a knot at one end of each piece of yarn. Have students hole-punch the sides of the hat and thread the yarn through. Invite students to wear their Rudolph hats while singing a favorite reindeer song.

MATERIALS
- Rudolph Hat pattern (page 76)
- large brown construction paper
- red, white, and black construction paper
- scissors
- glue

RUDOLPH MASKS

Have students trace one of their feet and both of their hands on brown construction paper and cut them out. Invite students to glue the handprint "antlers" to the back of the footprint "head." Students can decorate the reindeer face and glue on a pink cotton-ball nose.

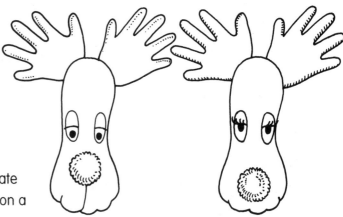

REINDEER SNACKS

Cut bread into triangles. Invite students to spread peanut butter on the triangles. Have students add a cherry nose, chocolate-chip eyes, and pretzel antlers. Enjoy!

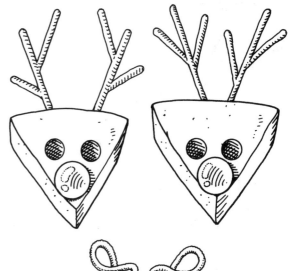

REINDEER LOLLIES

Invite each student to cover a lollipop with a fabric square. Ask students to tie a ribbon just under the "head" of the lollipop to secure the fabric. Invite students to glue on wiggly eyes, a pom-pom nose, and pipe-cleaner antlers to make a reindeer lolly.

RUDOLPH HAT

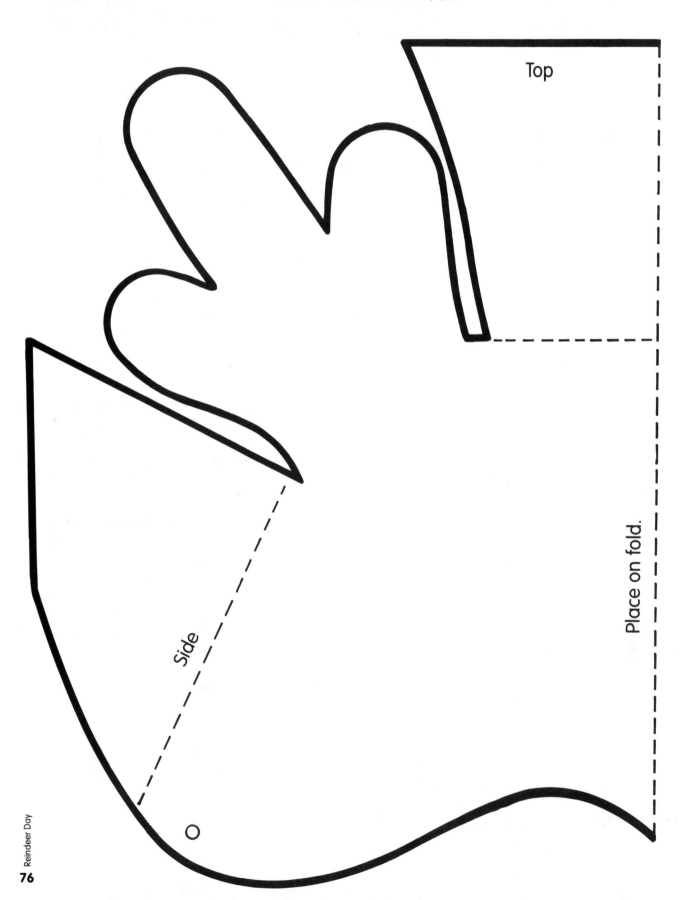

Top

Side

Place on fold.

December © 1998 Creative Teaching Press

CHRISTMAS

December 25

Christmas is the day Christians celebrate the birth of Jesus Christ, whom they believe to be the Son of God. Because the customs of the season are so widely followed, many people celebrate the positive spirit of the holiday even though they may not embrace its specific religious beliefs.

LITERATURE LINKS

Apple Tree Christmas
by Trinka Hakes Noble

*A Child Is Born:
The Christmas Story*
by Elizabeth Winthrop

The Christmas Alphabet
by Robert Sabuda

Corduroy's Christmas
by Don Freeman

The Crippled Lamb
by Max Lucado

An Early American Christmas
by Tomie dePaola

The Polar Express
by Chris Van Allsburg

THE 12 DAYS OF CHRISTMAS

Have the class write their own lyrics to "The 12 Days of Christmas" to make a fun holiday big book. Use the frame *On the _____ day of Christmas, my good friend gave to me _____* as a model. Have two or three students illustrate each page. Invite student groups to read and hold up one page. Bind the pages into a class big book.

MATERIALS
▲ large construction paper
▲ crayons or markers
▲ bookbinding materials

MATERIALS

▲ red construction paper or felt
▲ scissors
▲ curling ribbon
▲ old holiday greeting cards or gift wrap
▲ glue

HOLIDAY STOCKINGS

For each student, cut out two stocking shapes from red construction paper or felt. Punch holes around the edge of the stockings and have students stitch through the holes with curling ribbon. Invite students to cut up old Christmas cards or holiday wrapping paper to decorate the stocking. Display them on the bulletin board display described on page 24.

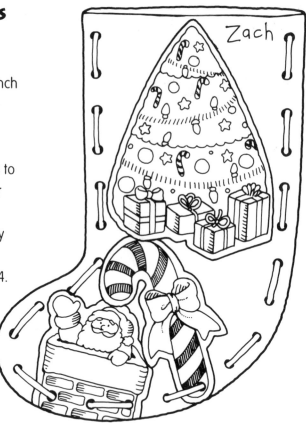

MATERIALS

▲ Three Kings reproducible (page 82)
▲ blue construction paper
▲ scissors
▲ glue
▲ fine and coarse sandpaper
▲ twine

THREE KINGS CARD

Have students fold blue construction paper in half to make a card. Ask students to color and cut out the patterns from the Three Kings reproducible and glue the star pattern to the top corner of their card. Invite each student to tear two hill patterns from fine sandpaper and one from coarse sandpaper. Invite students to glue one fine sandpaper hill below the star at the top of the card, overlap and glue the coarse sandpaper to the middle, and overlap and glue the other fine sandpaper at the bottom. Invite students to glue a twine "tail" to the back of each camel and glue the three kings and camels to the card, as shown. Students can draw a line from the king's hand to his camel. Have students write a holiday greeting inside, such as *These three kings traveled night and day to wish you a very special holiday!*

CHRISTMAS-TREE-LIGHT CARD

MATERIALS
▲ construction paper
▲ scissors
▲ black markers
▲ glue

Have students trace and cut out different-colored Christmas tree lights from construction paper. Invite students to draw a wavy black line on folded white construction paper. Have students glue their Christmas lights along the black line for a "string of lights" card. Have students write the following poem inside the card:

Twinkle, twinkle, little lights,
Shining on these holiday nights,
Lighting up the sky so bright,
Like a rainbow in the night.
Twinkle, twinkle, little lights,
Adding to the holiday sights!

BABY IN A MANGER CARD

MATERIALS
▲ blue, brown, yellow, and peach construction paper
▲ Manger Card reproducible (page 83)
▲ cheesecloth
▲ Spanish moss
▲ glue
▲ scissors
▲ glitter

Have students fold blue construction paper in half to make a card. Then have them trace the patterns from the Manger Card reproducible on construction paper and cut them out. Invite students to glue cheesecloth around the baby pattern and glue the baby's face to the body. Invite students to use markers to draw the baby's face. Invite students to sprinkle glitter on the star and halo patterns and then glue all the pieces to the card, as shown. Students can glue Spanish moss along the top of the manger. Have students write a holiday greeting inside.

THE GIVING TREE

MATERIALS
▲ artificial tree
▲ donations from families

Help a less fortunate family by asking your students' families to donate clothing and toys to a needy family. You can contact the police or Salvation Army to locate a needy family. Throughout the month, have students hang scarves, hats, mittens, toys, and other items on an artificial tree. Then at the end of the month, give the tree and all the gifts to the needy family. Invite students to write cards to the family members wishing them a happy holiday season.

CHRISTMAS ALPHABET BOOK

MATERIALS
▲ *The Christmas Alphabet* by Robert Sabuda
▲ drawing paper
▲ bookbinding materials

Read aloud *The Christmas Alphabet.* Discuss the different items that are associated with Christmas. Have students work in groups to create Christmas ABC books. Have students illustrate an item on each page. Bind pages together to make several class books.

GREEDY GIFTS GAME

MATERIALS
▲ computer paper writing paper
▲ drawing paper

Make an alphabetized list of gifts and write the list on a long scroll of computer paper. Tell a story about a greedy child who wanted many Christmas presents. Then read aloud the long list of all the desired gifts and show the class each word. After reading the list, give students writing paper and ask them to recall and write down as many of the listed gifts as possible. Invite volunteers to read their lists. Then, as a class, try to name each item in alphabetical order. Challenge students to make a list of nonmaterial gifts such as loves, smiles, and hugs.

THE NORTH POLE

MATERIALS

▲ *The Polar Express* by Chris Van Allsburg

▲ Train pattern (page 84)

▲ scissors

▲ blue construction paper

▲ sponges

▲ white paint

Read aloud and discuss *The Polar Express.* Ask students what they think it would be like to go to the North Pole. Have students write on the train pattern their journey to the North Pole and what they would like to give Santa. Have students cut out and glue the train on blue paper. Invite students to use sponges dipped in white paint to add "snow" to the paper.

TWENTY TURTLE DOVES

MATERIALS

▲ chart paper

▲ lyrics to "The 12 Days of Christmas"

List in a column on chart paper each gift item mentioned in the song "The 12 Days of Christmas." Write the numerals 1–12 across the top of the chart to represent the 12 days. Have students record day-by-day the total number of each gift given. Invite students to work in small groups to calculate the total number of gifts for each day and the grand total for the twelve-day period. Pose further questions for your students, such as *What was is the total number of gifts given for days three, four, and five?* or *How many fewer gifts were received on day six than on day twelve?* Invite students to use the chart to create their own questions.

	1	2	3	4	5	6	7	8	9
Partridge	1	1	1	1	1	1	1	1	1
Turtle doves		2	2	2	2	2	2	2	2
French hens			3	3	3	3	3	3	3
Calling birds				4	4	4	4	4	4
Golden rings					5	5	5	5	5
						6	6	6	6

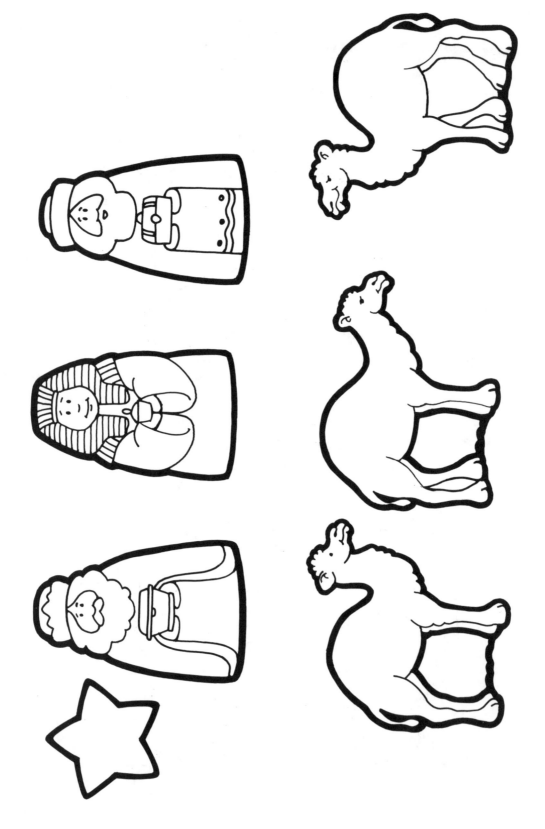

December © 1998 Creative Teaching Press

TRAIN

KWANZAA

Kwanzaa, a holiday that celebrates African American culture, was inspired by an ancient African harvest festival. In Swahili, Kwanzaa means *first fruits of the harvest.* Families gather each evening of Kwanzaa to light one of the seven candles in a kinara and talk about one of seven principles—unity, self-determination, collective work and responsibility, cooperative economics, purpose, creativity, and faith.

LITERATURE LINKS

Kwanzaa by A. P. Porter

Kwanzaa Celebration: Pop-up Book by Nancy Williams

My First Kwanzaa Book by Deborah M. Newton Chocolate

KWANZAA KINARA SNACK

The kinara is a candleholder used during Kwanzaa that holds three green candles, three red candles, and a black candle in the center. One candle is lit each day and each represents one of the seven principles. Invite students to make a simple treat in the shape of a kinara. Give each student half a pita pocket and have students spread cream cheese inside the pocket. Then give each student three celery sticks and three carrot sticks to place inside as candles. Have students place black licorice in the center. Enjoy!

MATERIALS
▲ pita bread
▲ cream cheese
▲ plastic knives
▲ celery sticks
▲ carrot sticks
▲ black licorice

DASHIKI SHIRTS

A dashiki is a loose, colorful shirt worn by Africans at the karamu, or Kwanzaa feast. Students can make a simple version from paper grocery sacks. Have students cut along the seams of a paper grocery sack until they have a long piece of brown paper. Have students cut out a neck hole and a slit down the front from the neck. Invite students to decorate their dashiki with rows of painted Kwanzaa symbols such as straw mats; unity cups; black, red, and green candles; ears of corn; kinaras (seven-candle candleholders); and fruits and vegetables. Help students staple the sides, leaving room for the arms. Invite students to sing "Kwanzaa" while they wear their dashiki shirts.

Kwanzaa

(to the tune of "Bingo")

There is a holiday I know, and Kwanzaa is its name, oh
Candle lights and food so good,
All around my neighborhood,
Love and thanks for all that's good.
And Kwanzaa is its name, oh.

MATERIALS

▲ Heritage Shield reproducible (page 88)

▲ crayons or markers

HERITAGE SHIELDS

Africans once used shields as part of a warrior's costume, but today shields are used primarily as a reminder of African heritage. Invite students to bring in a family photograph, something that tells about them, and a drawing of what they would like to be when they grow up. Have students decorate the Heritage Shield reproducible with these important clues to their heritage and goals. Ask students to write the "seven principle" words around the perimeter of the shield.

MATERIALS

▲ red, green, and black construction paper

▲ scissors

WOVEN MKEKA MATS

A mkeka is a woven straw mat that represents the traditions and history of African Americans. Other Kwanzaa symbols are placed on the mkeka. To make a mkeka, students first make a weaving sheet by folding construction paper in half widthwise and cutting a line every inch (2.5 cm), beginning at the folded edge and stopping one inch (2.5 cm) from the ends of the paper. Make weaving strips by cutting one-inch (2.5-cm) strips across the width of construction paper. To weave, invite students to use one of the strips to slide over and then under the slats of the weaving sheet. Have students repeat with another strip, weaving the opposite way (first under, then over). Encourage students to make patterns with the Kwanzaa colors—green (symbolizing the promise of youth), red (symbolizing the struggle of African Americans), and black (symbolizing Americans of African descent). When all the strips have been woven, have students glue the ends to the weaving sheet to secure them.

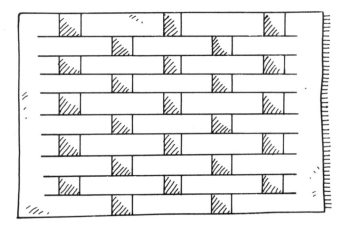

HERITAGE SHIELD

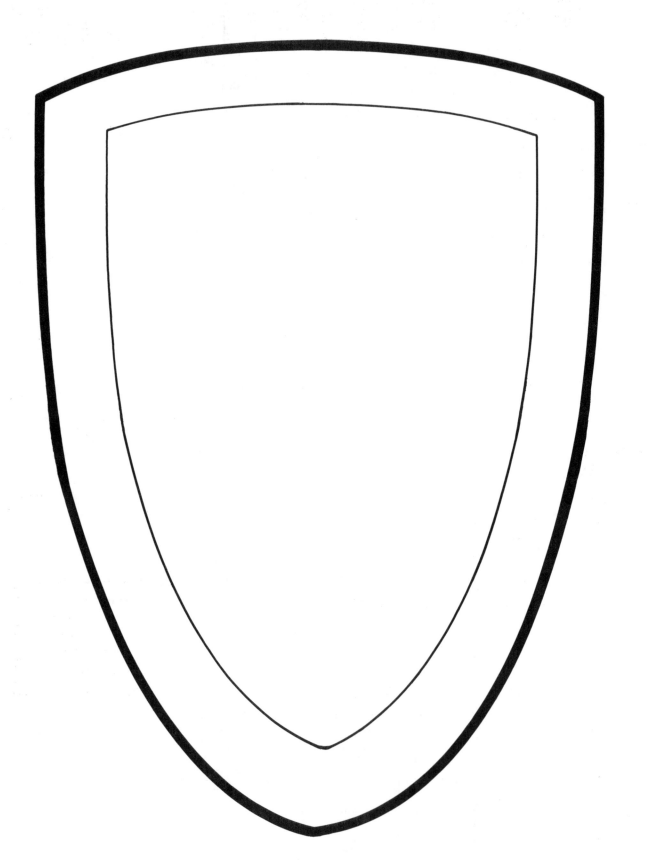

JUST SO STORIES DAY

December 30

Rudyard Kipling was born on this day in Bombay, India. His *Just So Stories* have delighted generations of children. Introduce your students to these irresistible tales!

LITERATURE LINKS

Books by Rudyard Kipling

Beginning of the Armadillos

The Cat That Walked by Himself

The Crab That Played with the Sea

The Elephant's Child

How the Camel Got His Hump

How the Leopard Got His Spots

How the Rhinoceros Got His Skin

The Jungle Book

Just So Stories

Rikki-Tikki-Tavi

Before the Zebra Got Its Stripes

Timm

"HOW IT HAPPENED" ILLUSTRATIONS

Read a few stories from *Just So Stories.* Have students imagine and then illustrate how an animal looks before it gets its distinguishing features. For example, have students draw a camel before it acquires a hump or a giraffe before it grows a long neck. Invite students to share their drawings and tell their versions of how the animals eventually acquire their traits.

MATERIALS

▲ *Just So Stories* by Rudyard Kipling

▲ crayons or markers

▲ drawing paper

JUST SO STORIES

Read one or more of Kipling's *Just So Stories,* such as "How the Camel Got His Hump." Have students brainstorm a list of animals and write them on paper. Ask students to write beside each animal one or more of its outstanding characteristics, such as giraffe/neck, shark/teeth, beaver/tail, mouse/ears, tiger/stripes. Invite students to choose one of the animals to write their own "just so story" about.

How the Parrot Got Its Beautiful Wings
by Elgin
One day a parrot flew through a rainbow.

CURIOSITY CAPERS

Read aloud and discuss *The Elephant's Child.* Discuss with students the trait of curiosity. Have students use the Elephant reproducible to tell about a time when their curiosity got them into or helped them stay out of trouble. Have students accordion-fold the trunk, glue it to the elephant, and color the elephant. Display the elephants on a bulletin board titled *Curiosity Capers.*

I saw a small bug on the ground and I just had to touch it. When I did, I was sorry. I got stung by it. It was a bee.
Joey

TRIP TO THE JUNGLE

Ask students to rest their heads and close their eyes as you read the following guided-imagery script.

> *Imagine you are in a hot, humid jungle. There are green trees and bushes everywhere. Leafy vines brush against you as you walk through the bushes. The sounds of monkeys and birds fill the air. You see a snake slithering off in the distance. You hear a lion roar, and your heart leaps as you see him jump off a tree branch and walk over to a cool pool.*

After listening, students can write their own jungle books or continue from where you stopped.

ELEPHANT

Just So Stories Day

DECEMBER

SUNDAY	MONDAY	TUESDAY	WEDNESDAY	THURSDAY	FRIDAY	SATURDAY

December Calendar